CISTERCIAN FATHERS SERIES: NUMBER SIXTY-THREE

Gertrud the Great of Helfta

THE HERALD OF GOD'S LOVING-KINDNESS: BOOK THREE

CISTERCIAN FATHERS SERIES: NUMBER SIXTY-THREE

GERTRUD THE GREAT OF HELFTA

THE HERALD OF GOD'S LOVING-KINDNESS: BOOK THREE

Translated, with an introduction and notes, by
Alexandra Barratt

Cistercian Publications
Kalamazoo, Michigan

Cistercian Publications Inc.
Editorial Office
The Institute of Cistercian Studies
Western Michigan University
Kalamazoo, MI 49008

Distribution Offices
Saint Joseph's Abbey
Spencer, MA 01562

Mount Saint Bernard Abbey
Coalville, Leicester LE67 5UL

The work of Cistercian Publications
is made possible in part by support from Western Michigan University
to The Institute of Cistercian Studies

Library of Congress Cataloguing-in-Publication Data
is available upon request.

Printed in the United States of America

TABLE OF CONTENTS

INTRODUCTION

GERTRUD THE GREAT (1256–1302) spent virtually all her life as a benedictine nun at the monastery of Helfta, in Upper Saxony.[1] She entered as a child ('less than five years old' I.1.1, 'scarcely weaned', I.1.2) and received a thorough education in the liberal arts, including the study of Latin, and in the scriptures. At the age of twenty-five[2] she was underwent a conversion and for the rest of her life experienced visions, many of them relating to the divine Heart.[3] Consequently she is often regarded as an important precursor of devotion to the Sacred Heart.[4] But she was also a prolific writer and her name is associated with several

[1] Technically, Helfta was a benedictine monastery. It was however strongly influenced by the cistercian reform and the nuns wore the cistercian habit of unbleached wool. See further Caroline Bynum Walker, *Jesus As Mother: Studies in the Spirituality of the High Middle Ages* (Berkeley and Los Angeles: University of California Press, 1982) 174–5 and the references given there.

[2] It may be significant that in the middle ages it was not until the age of twenty-five that a nun could receive the consecration of a virgin: see *Gertrud the Great of Helfta: Spiritual Exercises*. Translation, introduction, notes and indexes by Gertrud Jaron Lewis and Jack Lewis, Cistercian Fathers Series No. 49 (Kalamazoo: Cistercian Publications, 1989) 14.

[3] For further information about Gertrud's life and the history of Helfta, see *The Herald of God's Loving-Kindness Books One & Two*, translated and annotated by Alexandra Barratt, Cistercian Fathers Series No. 35 (Kalamazoo: Cistercian Publications, 1991) 7–12.

[4] See further *The Herald . . . Books One & Two*, 19–25 for an account of Gertrud's theology of the divine Heart and her place in the development of the cult of the Sacred Heart.

texts: the *Spiritual Exercises*, the *Book of Special Grace* of Mechtild of Hackeborn, which Gertrud probably helped to compile, and above all *The Herald of God's Loving-Kindness*, which consists in all of five books: Book One a biographical study, Book Two written by Gertrud herself, and Books Three, Four and Five compiled at her direction and under her supervision by another nun.

Elsewhere I have, perhaps rashly, described Gertrud as 'the most literary of all the medieval women visionaries'.[5] In part, of course, this refers to the many texts of which, in one sense or another, she was the author. But it also points to her pervasive, and self-conscious, concern with a whole range of activities involved in text-production: reading, writing, the varied technologies of literacy, even the abstract and sophisticated question of the differences between oral and written communication.

The Herald itself is what modern critics would call a 'self-referential' text. Its Prologue carefully, if confusingly, records in some detail when, in what order, and why the different books and even the two subdivisions of Book Two were composed. It also explains the various titles bestowed on the different parts by the Lord (Prologue, 1-7). Book One goes on to make many references to Gertrud's literary skills, as writer, compiler, editor, transcriber, interpreter and even, when necessary, as censor (e.g. I.1.2; I.4.2; I.6.1; I.7.1; I.8.1; I.9.1). Book Two exposes in passing the literate environment at Helfta: there are frequent references to the reading and chanting of the divine office from liturgical books, to books of edification or of private devotion, to other written documents, and equipment for writing such as the tablet Gertrud apparently always carried with her (I.11.10; II.Prologue), and her pencil (I.13.4), which she often dropped. Moreover that Gertrud's own mentality had been thoroughly permeated by literacy is clear from the many metaphors she uses based on the experiences of reading and writing. (One of the most interesting occurs in Book Three (30.40) where the Lord compares his teaching of patience to a teacher teaching a child the alphabet.) But she was not so modern as to miss the profound differences between oral and

[5] *Women's Writing in Middle English*, edited by Alexandra Barratt, Longman Annotated Texts (London and New York: Longman, 1992) 49.

written communication (II.10.1). She knew that written texts both substitute for and supplement the memory and have a unique power to recall events from the past. Perhaps she forfeited the slippages and flexbilities of oral discourse, but she gained permanence and definition from her capacity to write in Latin. More than the many medieval women visionaries who were dependent on male clerics as scribes and editors, Gertrud could herself write what she wanted posterity to read in Book Two of *The Herald*, and could presumably monitor the way in which her own experiences were represented in Books Three, Four and Five.

ORIGINS AND STRUCTURE OF BOOK 3

Book Three of *The Herald of God's Loving-Kindness*, unlike Book Two which records experiences that Gertrud 'described with her own hand', was compiled twenty years later by another member of the Helfta community. Possibly this was the same nun who, after Gertrud's death, wrote the biographical study that constitutes Book One. As we are told in the Prologue to Book Three, 'The grace of great humility, together with the swiftly compelling power of the divine will, led [Gertrud] to convey all that follows to a certain person . . . that person wrote down what follows under obedience to the commands of her superiors'. Consequently Book Three lacks the immediacy and authenticity of Book Two, nor does it have the elaborate artificial structure of the biographical Book One.[6] Indeed, it is quite accurately if baldly characterized in the Prologue to the entire treatise: 'The third book expounds something of the favors lavished on or revealed to her'. (Prologue.6)

Like many women visionaries, Gertrud was reluctant to communicate her intimate experiences of the divine even in this filtered and indirect fashion. It needed the direct orders of both the Blessed Virgin Mary and the Lord to persuade her to 'disclose whatever [he] had conferred on her' (III.1.2). An experience recorded in Book Three was clearly a turning-point in this regard. In Chapter 30 we

[6]See *The Herald . . . Books One & Two*, 15–17.

are told how she came to understand her vocation as a mediator of the divine Heart:

> . . . she offered the Lord her own heart. . . . The Son of God appeared, offering God the Father her heart united with his own divine Heart. . . . When she saw this she said to the Lord with suppliant devotion, 'Most loving God, grant that my heart may be always at hand . . . so that you may always, as you please, have it clean for pouring in and pouring out whenever you wish, for whomever you please'.
>
> The Son of God kindly accepted this and said to the Father, 'Holy Father, may this heart pour out, to your eternal praise, all that my Heart contained for dispensation in my human nature'. . . . she understood from this time on that it was the Lord's pleasure that she should have such things written down for the profit of many. (III.30.2)

Book Three gives the impression of having been put together over a period of time from notes or fragments. It has no obvious structure or narrative thread, and the most one can say is that it consists of groups of chapters clustered according to common themes or connected by similar circumstances. Indeed another modern translation makes clear its view that Book Three lacks organic unity by omitting without apology 'certain chapters of lesser interest or importance, or which contain duplication of material found elsewhere'.[7] The work is divided into two unequal parts: the first consists of Chapters 1–65 and the second of Chapters 66–89. Many of the revelations and spiritual colloquies recorded in the first part of Book Three are liturgical in inspiration, linked to the mass, reception of the sacrament of communion, or the recitation of the divine office (Chapters 4–38). Chapters 39–47 focus in various ways on the remembrance of Christ's Passion, Chapters 50–64 are linked by the theme of the visionary's sickness, while Chapter 65 ends this

[7] *Gertrude of Helfta: The Herald of Divine Love.* Trans. and ed. by Margaret Winkworth. Intro. by Sister Maximillian Marnau. Preface by Louis Bouyer. Classics of Western Spirituality (Paulist Press: New York and Mahwah, NJ, 1993) 3. The translation omits Chapters 3, 12, 13, 15, 21, 24, 27, 29, 31, 34, 37, 39, 45, 47, 49, 54, 58, 62, 66, 71–3, 75 to the end.

part of Book Three with a lengthy and rhapsodic prose-poem in praise of Christ.

The shorter section from Chapter 66 onwards is accurately if briefly summarized in the text itself as 'some things . . . which God revealed to her when she was praying for certain people' (III.66). In this part of the book Gertrud's role is compared with that of a water pipe in mediating the stream of graces from the divine Heart to others, both within and without the Helfta community.

CONTENT AND THEMES

If Book Three is a less than cohesive and satisfying whole, this is quite possibly deliberate. The text presents the Lord himself as having pre-empted the imposition of any single unified reading, when he declared to Gertrud that 'it is necessary that different people should find in your book different things suited to them for their own instruction and consolation' (III.64.3). None the less the text is immediately attractive as it contains many vivid, even startling, analogies (*similitudines*), often taken from the noble life of the high middle ages.[8] One also gains a lively sense of the Helfta community and its world: of the nuns themselves, their relatives and friends (III.30.38 and 79.1), their priests and confessors (notable by their absence in III.60.1 and 61.1); the lay servants of the monastery (III.68.1), and even their secular enemies (III.67.1). The nuns include the learned woman who can read and study Scripture and the unlearned sister who cooks the meals (III.73.12), the superiors with their inevitable shortcomings (III.82.1) and the conscientious hebdomadaries (III.80.1 and 81.1). Among the community's activities are hearing sermons and the preaching of indulgences (III.11.1, 18.13, 20.1, 51.1) and taking part in processions (III.31.1). There are also traces of Helfta's eventful external history, notably the interdict under which it suffered (III.16.1), a threatened armed attack (III.48.1), rough weather (III.31.1 and 2), the stress caused

[8]Sister Mary Jeremy's classic article, '"Similitudes" in the Writing of Saint Gertrude of Helfta', *Mediaeval Studies* 19 (1957) 48–54, is still a valuable introduction to this aspect of Gertrud's writings.

by its unpaid debts (III.68.1–4), and its plans for a new foundation (III.64.1).

Gertrud's own life, when she is not sick, is largely one of liturgical and private prayer and of study. Chanting or at least reciting the divine office decently and with proper care and concentration was of great importance to her (III.25.1; III.84.1). But there are also references to her participation in household tasks. We see her spinning—rather clumsily, one gathers (III.32.4)—just as Book One included references to her sewing and her tendency to drop her needle (I.13.4). Either she or her amanuensis had been in a kitchen often enough to compare the inevitable benefits of devotion to Christ's Passion to the disconcerting way in which 'it is impossible for anyone to touch flour without getting dusty' (III.41.4).

But insights into life in a benedictine convent in medieval Saxony are merely incidental. There are serious spiritual themes present in Book Three, even if they are not developed systematically for Gertrud was temperamentally a poet rather than a theologian, and works on her readers by imagery and allusion, not by logical exposition.

SICKNESS, SUFFERING AND EVIL[9]

Gertrud was repeatedly unwell and not surprisingly the text has much to say about suffering, both physical and mental. We know little of the specificities of her situation except that among other complaints she suffered from frequent fevers (III.53.1), was confined to bed on at least seven occasions (III.55.1), and had a painful left eye. The Lord had anointed this in a vision with a betrothal ring representing physical suffering and she regarded this as 'a most certain sign of divine election' (III.2.1). She also experienced much mental anguish—described in one instance as 'darkness, as a result of a certain disordered depression together with impatience' (III.2.1)—sometimes from specific causes, sometimes apparently spontaneous.

[9]See Bynum, *Jesus As Mother*, 191–196, for a somewhat different perspective on Gertrud, suffering and evil.

When she prays for release from pain the Lord refuses, replying, 'Do you not know that I look upon you with my most merciful gaze because you are physically chastised and mentally distressed?' (III.30.12). But it is not her mental and physical suffering in itself that is meritorious so much as her acceptance of it as divinely willed (III.4.1). Sickness cannot be an excuse either for slackness (she continues to say the Hours as well as she can, III.59.1) or for masochistic asceticism (III.22.1). Nor should it force her to abandon contemplation in favor of strict observance of the Rule (III.44.2), even though her friends advise her to do so (III.54.1). The Lord dismisses her requests to be restored to health in order to follow the Rule more devoutly as 'girlish chatter' and she realizes that 'it is far more perfect for a person to entrust himself completely to the divine will, in full trust that whatever fate God ordains for him, whether better or worse, is the most healthy for that individual' (III.50.3).

Gertrud deals with evil, as distinct from suffering, under two aspects. Abstract evil is manifested in the Devil. When he mocks her for reciting the psalms without due care and attention he is presented not as terrifying but as petty and malicious: 'the cunning enemy had so carefully counted up the individual sounds and syllables . . . that he could bring a serious charge after death against those who are in the habit of saying the Hours hastily' (III.32.4). But he is merely ridiculous when he tries to get her into trouble for dropping balls of wool while spinning (III.32.5) or is burnt by the grape skins he has been collecting as evidence that the visionary had eaten before Matins:

> He had scarcely touched one of the bits of skin with a couple of fingers when he was consumed by a fire of unbearable torture. Letting out terrible shrieks he bounded out of the room, taking the greatest care not to let his feet touch any more bits, from contact with which he had experienced the torture of such unbearable pain. (III.57.2)

On the other hand, Gertrud learns to be reluctant to pass any kind of judgment on apparent evil manifested in human form: when she asks the Lord how those who placed the monastery under an interdict could continue to possess his grace she is firmly warned off the subject: 'The Lord said, 'Let it be. I shall deal with them in this matter' (III.16.3). Instead, she is shown that the enemies of Helfta are still members of the Body of Christ, even if currently excommunicated, and that to treat them harshly or wish them ill is therefore to maltreat Christ himself: the Lord condemns 'all those who, with no pity for the damnation of souls that those who attack my own people risk, wickedly proclaim over and over again those people's failings and the injuries inflicted on themselves, not remembering that those people too are my members'. (III.67.1–2, cf. III.74.1–2)

THE INDIVIDUAL AND THE COMMUNITY

In Gertrud's thought, the individual and the community receive equal emphasis and coexist in balanced harmony. Her own relationship with God is intensely individual and presented metaphorically under various guises (child and parent, bride and bridegroom) that stress its unique personal nature. She also continually emphasizes the organic nature of the Church as Body of Christ, and the corporate nature of her own religious community as its microcosm.[10] We see Helfta acting together as a community, coordinating prayers for souls in purgatory (III.9.1). Gertrud herself becomes aware that the Lord is distributing these prayers and at his prompting she offers up as her own contribution the merits of her community: 'I offer you, Lord, not only my own spiritual possessions, which are worth next to nothing, but also those of the whole community from the common life which I share with them, claiming them as my own in their entirety, through your grace' (III.9.1). As a natural corollary all members of the Helfta community benefit spiritually from the privileges of the few: the Lord explains to her that

> when a person eats, by which the whole body is strengthened in every individual member, nevertheless only the mouth delights in the taste of the food. In the same way, when a special

[10]Bynum comments that Gertrud 'had a strong sense of community', *Jesus as Mother*, 195.

> grace is granted to those who have been chosen, out of God's unrestrained loving-kindness merit also increases for all members [of the Church] and especially for those belonging to the same community, with the exception of those who deprive themselves of it through envy and ill-will. (III.17.3)

Logically, then, the deficiencies of one sister cancel out those of another to achieve a balanced whole. Explaining how one sister may be too timid to receive communion while another is too precipitate, the Lord asks:

> Do you not consider that I am owed no less justly the reverence of honor than the sweetness of love? But . . . since you are members one of another it is right that what someone lacks in herself should be recovered by another. For instance, someone who with too much sweet love yields to less feeling of reverence should rejoice that this is made up for her by another who extends greater reverence. (III.18.19)

Just because of this corporate nature, the duty of correction within the community must not be shirked.[11] Gertrud herself shrank from getting a bad reputation as over-zealous in correcting others: indeed, we know from an episode recounted in Book One (12.1) that some of her sisters did think she was sometimes too harsh in her rebukes. But the Lord told her that she would be rewarded for enduring such criticism (III.62.1). She clearly knew that correcting one's fellows could be a thankless and frustrating task (III.74.3):

> Again, from the verse 'Where is your brother Abel?' she understood that the Lord requires from every religious anything done by a neighbor against religion, whose prevention he could somehow have effected. . . . That excuse some people make—'It is not my job to correct others' and 'I myself am worse than him'—does as little good before God as it did Cain, who said, 'Am I my brother's keeper?' For everyone is bound in the eyes of God to restrain his brother from evil and urge him on to good. . . . Nor does it do any good that he claims it has not been entrusted to him, for this has indeed been entrusted to

[11] This is a characteristically cistercian theme: see Bynum, *Jesus As Mother*, 68.

> him; beyond that, his own conscience shows him. (III.30.18; cf. III.74.2)

Such correction must be carried out with discretion (III.78.1) and in particular should not be too harsh, for 'if too much is said the words call forth God's mercy and become increase of the guilty one's merit.' (III.30.11)

The individual within the community retains spiritual autonomy. She is not only, of course, responsible for her own failings, but her spiritual privileges are, as it were, tailor-made by the Lord, bearing in mind her own particular psychological and spiritual constitution. When she asks, 'Why, most loving Lord, are those things that you condescend by your generous loving-kindness to reveal to me quite frequently so different from the revelations of others?' the Lord stresses in his reply his own freedom of action both in granting revelations and in adapting them to the individual: 'I reveal what I want, according to a person's intellectual capacity with which I have endowed him, that is, by showing things to the more simple through largely physical analogies, and to the more intellectually capable by expounding more hidden and obscure shadowy sketches' (III.48.2). This also applies to other graces. In an implicit recognition that everyone is different, the Lord explains to Gertrud why the love of some of the sisters has grown cold under the interdict: 'I contain every good thing in myself and to each at the ordained time I give a part suited to the individual.' (III.16.5)

THE SACRAMENTAL LIFE

That so many of Gertrud's revelations and colloquies take place in the context of the liturgy is indicative of the supreme importance the sacramental life had for her. She places her greatest stress on the sacrament of communion. Simple attendance at the Eucharist, while necessary, is far outweighed by the value she (and the Lord) place on the frequent reception of communion (see III.10.1–2, 36 and 77 and also I.14.2). In this she is unlike many of her medieval contemporaries. The minimum obligation for all Christians at the time was to make their confession and communion once a year at

Easter, and this was not often exceeded. The extreme reverence the middle ages felt for the consecrated host was encouraged by the institution in the thirteenth century of the feast of Corpus Christi and resulted from theological debates over the doctrine of transubstantiation. That Helfta shared this awe is evident from the consternation caused when a host, which may or may not have been consecrated, is found caught in the altar hangings (III.13.1). Consequently medieval people placed tremendous emphasis on careful preparation for the worthy reception of the sacrament, to such an extent that frequent communion was uncommon and even, out of the best of motives, discouraged.

Gertrud however constantly stresses the need for trust in God's mercy (*confidentia*: cf. III.17.2) and this is collaborated by her biographer who devotes a whole chapter to 'Her Gift of Trust for Which She was Famous' (I.10). She herself models confident reception of communion combined with an acceptance—indeed, a joyful acceptance—of one's unworthiness:

> One day when she was about to receive communion, when she thought she was not prepared and the time was already at hand, she said to her soul, 'Here is the bridegroom already calling you, and how can you go to meet him, not prepared with any adornment of suitable merits?' Then pondering again much more on her own unworthiness, completely distrusting herself and putting her hope in God's loving-kindness, she said to herself, 'What's the use of putting it off? Even if I were left to my own efforts for a thousand years, I would not prepare myself suitably; since I can have nothing of myself which can in any way lead to such a costly preparation. But I shall go to meet him with humility and trust.' (III.18.10)

Apart from Chapter 60, in which the Lord raises all seven sacraments to a spiritual plane, Gertrud has little to say about the others, even that of penance. This is perhaps because she does not seem to be excessively burdened with a sense of sin, as distinct from a tendency to scrupulosity. She frequently refers to her 'faults' (*culpae*) and her 'failings', 'negligences', or sins of omission. But the only positive sin with which she repeatedly berates herself is that of impatience. There are several references to occasions on which she could not make her confession because there was no confessor available, but in fact only one chapter deals with the subject of making confession. Chapter 14 contains a lengthy description of an occasion on which she found the prospect of confession so daunting that she was consoled by the Lord with an elaborate analogy of confession as a healing bath. All the same 'her confession was a great burden to her, so much so that she labored with the greatest difficulty in mentioning those things which some people do not blush to proclaim before everyone, as if they were boasting'. (III.14.3)

HUMILITY[12]

Book Three makes no reference to any supernatural privileges enjoyed by Gertrud other than the revelations themselves and the relationship with the divine of which they are a manifestation. As Sister Maximillian Marnau has acutely observed, 'We do not, indeed, get the impression that Gertrude was externally unusual except in her wholeheartedness and her wisdom; her mystical experiences do not seem . . . to have intruded in her life and may perhaps have been quite unknown to most of her sisters'.[13] Although her biographer gives several examples in Book One of occasions on which God 'fulfilled her predictions and made known all her secret insights' (I.2.2–4), Gertrud is no thaumaturge and she herself never claims privileged knowledge. On the contrary: the text is so concerned to stress her humility that from time to time the reader's attention is sedulously drawn to her divinely-imposed limitations. For instance, the Lord will not tell her how long the monastery will be under the interdict, although she asks outright. Nor, out of 'the fatherly foresight of [his] uncreated wisdom' (III.55.2), will he tell her whether or not her seventh attack of sickness will be her last, or what the ultimate outcome will be (III.56.1). Indeed he explains

[12]On this theme in Gertrud's writings, see Michael Bangert, *Demut in Freiheit: Studien zur geistlichen Lehre im Werk Gertruds von Helfta*. Studien zur systematischen und spirituellen Theologie, 21 (Würzburg: Echter Verlag, 1997).

[13]*Gertrude of Helfta: The Herald*, 42.

that he sometimes deliberately excludes her from his confidences not because she is, as she claims, 'one of the lowest of the low' or 'the dregs of . . . creation' (III.16.1) but in order to safeguard her humility. And it is to that humility that we owe the very existence of Book Three: as we have already seen,[14] the opening words of the Prologue relate how it was '[t]he grace of great humility' that led her to convey to its compiler the experiences that it details.

It is hard to capture the essential quality of Book Three. But the experiences that it contains, however fragmentary, elusive, enigmatic and even random they may seem at times, have been aptly characterized as 'a detailed record of God's dealings with a soul'.[15] In the last analysis, perhaps, it is to study those dealings as they unfold day by day in the ordered life of a woman separated from us in time by seven hundred years, in space by many thousands of miles, but at least no longer by a foreign language, that this book has been translated and, it is to be hoped, will be read.

[14]See above, p. 11.

[15]*Gertrude of Helfta: The Herald*, 29.

THE HERALD OF GOD'S LOVING-KINDNESS: BOOK THREE

PROLOGUE

THE GRACE OF GREAT HUMILITY, together with the swiftly compelling power of the divine will, led her to convey all that follows to a certain person. This she did because she thought herself unworthy, as her gratitude was by no means sufficient to respond to the greatness of God's gifts. For this reason when she made these revelations to another person she rejoiced in the praise of God which, at that time, was in her view like a jewel which had been raised from dark mud and placed in a lofty setting of shining gold. Subsequently that person wrote down what follows under obedience to the commands of her superiors.

CHAPTER ONE

SPECIAL CARE FROM THE MOTHER OF GOD

1. When she had understood from a spiritual revelation that some misfortune was threatening that would increase her merit, and consequently shrank from it through human weakness, the kind and loving Lord, coming down to the level of her faintheartedness, appointed his merciful Mother, glorious Empress of Heaven, as her kindly guardian.[1] As a result, whenever she was weighed down by some excessive trouble beyond her powers, she might always have confident recourse to that Mother of mercy, through whose intervention she knew she would receive relief.

2. A short time after this she was greatly weighed down because someone devoted to God compelled her to disclose whatever the Lord had conferred on her as a special gift at the preceding feast. For various reasons she considered it very difficult to do this at that time. If, however, she refused altogether, she was afraid of going against God's will. She ran to the comforter of the desolate, longing to learn from her what was the better course of action in this situation. She received this reply from her: 'Pay out what you have, for my son has riches enough to repay whatever you pay out in his praise'.

[1] *dispensatricem*, literally 'female steward'.

But since she had hedged around her secret with so many barriers of her own devising that only with the greatest difficulty could she bring herself to disclose it, for that very reason she flung herself in supplication at the feet of the Lord, that he might make known to her what would better please him and provide her with the will to carry it out. Hence by his kindness she merited to be assured by such an answer: 'Give my money to the money-lender's table so that when I return I may demand it with interest'.[2] In this way she learnt that those promptings which she thought rational and sent her by the Holy Spirit had in fact sprung from a human root, her own personal opinion. Hence from that time forward she began to relax the rigor of her intention—rightly so, for as Solomon bears witness, 'The glory of kings is to conceal the word; but the glory of God is to search out the speech'.[3]

[2]Lk 19:23.

[3]Cf. Prv 25:2; this text is also misquoted by Bernard of Clairvaux, SC 65:3.

CHAPTER TWO

THE RINGS OF HER SPIRITUAL BETROTHAL

1. While she was offering up to the Lord in a prayer all the suffering that weighed upon her both in body and in spirit, and all the pleasure of which she was deprived both in the spirit and in the flesh, the Lord appeared wearing on both hands those two offerings which she had made him—that is, pleasure and suffering—like ornaments in the shape of jeweled rings. When she had understood this, she repeated the previous prayer again. A little later, while she was reciting it she sensed the Lord Jesus was anointing her left eye with the ring on his left hand, which she had understood to represent physical suffering. Then that same eye, which the Lord seemed to have touched in spirit, became physically painful, so much so that afterwards it never completely recovered its former health. From this she understood that, just as a ring is a sign of betrothal, so misfortune, both physical and spiritual, is a most certain sign of divine election and is, so to speak, the soul's betrothal to God; so much so that everyone who is weighed down may truly, or rather confidently, say this: 'My lord Jesus Christ has plighted his troth to me with his ring'.[1] And if, amidst one's troubles, one does not lack this gift—that is, one can raise up the mind to God in praise and

[1] Office of Saint Agnes, Vespers antiphon.

gratitude—consequently one can go further with delight and say this: 'Moreover he has adorned me as his bride with a crown'. For in time of trouble gratitude is the most splendid crown of glory, incomparably more valuable than gold and topaz.[2]

[2]Ps 118:127.

CHAPTER THREE

THE DIGNITY OF SUFFERING

1. She received indisputable evidence that the opposite of pleasure in hardship is the increase of glory, which she had not understood until then. One day around the feast of Pentecost she was so unbearably tormented by a pain in her side that those near her would have reckoned it more easy for her to die on that day rather than survive, if they had not known that she had quite often recovered from similar pain. Her kindly lover and her soul's true comforter gave her this recompense: that whenever she lay there, suffering want from the negligence of those serving her, the kind and loving Lord himself appeared, whose soothing presence mitigated her pain. But when care of her helpers was more attentive, the Lord stole away and the pain grew more oppressive. By this she was clearly given to understand that the more one is abandoned by human beings, the more one is regarded by the divine mercy.

And when the day was drawing near evening and she suffered an excruciating attack, she tried to persuade the Lord that her pain should be relieved. The Lord raised his arms and showed her that he wore on his breast, like a jewel, the pain she had endured during the day. Now when she saw that jewel, which seemed perfect and completely flawless, she rejoiced and hoped that from then on her pain would cease. To this the Lord answered: 'Whatever you suffer from now onwards will add glory to this jewel'. For although it was studded with gems, still it seemed less radiant, like gold grown dim.[1]

Her next source of suffering was the plague, which she now contracted. She was not seriously ill but was wearied more by absence of pleasure than sharpness of pain.

[1]Lam 4:1.

CHAPTER FOUR

CONTEMPT FOR WORLDLY CONVENIENCE

1. Around the feast of Saint Bartholomew[1] she fell into such darkness, as a result of a certain disordered depression together with impatience, that it seemed to her that she had largely lost the delight of the presence of God, until one Saturday she rejoiced to see the clouds of darkness moderated by the intervention of the Virgin Mother of God when the antiphon 'Mary, star of the sea' was being sung in her honor. On the following Sunday, when she was rejoicing that God in his kindliness was caring so gently for her, and was recalling her past impatience and her other failings, she became extremely annoyed with herself and began to implore the Lord, with great dejection of spirit, to correct her. As if because of the great number and extent of the failings that she had detected in herself, in near-desperation she said to the Lord, 'Ah, most merciful Lord, put an end to my evil deeds, in which I apply neither limit nor end. Free me and place me at your side, and no one's hand may be against me'.[2]

The kindly Lord took pity on her desolation and showed her a garden, very small and extremely narrow, full of all kinds of flowers

[1] 24 August.

[2] Jb 17:3.

in bloom, which was fenced around with thorns and had a tiny stream of honey flowing through it. He said to her, 'Would you prefer that pleasure which you could enjoy among those beautiful flowers to me?' She replied, 'No indeed, Lord God'. Then he showed her a muddy little garden, but covered with a meager amount of green growth, having here and there a few tiny flowers of no value but a little color. He asked her the same question about this and said, 'Surely you would not prefer these things to me?' She turned away from it angrily and said, 'Far be it from my soul that I should prefer something false and worthless, not good but evil, to you the only Truth, the greatest, the constant, steadfast and everlasting Good'.

The Lord said, 'Why then do you doubt whether you are in charity, in which anyone is proved to be who abounds in so many good things and since, as Scripture witnesses, "Charity covers a multitude of sins"[3]? This is why you did not prefer to my will your own, according to which you could live an easy, honorable life, without any trouble, finding favor in human eyes and a reputation for every kind of holiness. For this was what I showed you in the likeness of the flowering garden, and I offered you the pleasure of a fleshly life in the green growth of that muddy place'. She replied, 'How I wish—how many thousand times I wish—that in that worthless little flower-garden you showed me I had completely renounced my own will! But I am afraid it was its narrowness that persuaded me to spurn it the more easily'.

The Lord replied, 'Thus is the abundance of my loving-kindness accustomed to constrict worldly conveniences through remorse of conscience for all those whom he has chosen, so that they may quite easily hold them cheap'. Then she, renouncing all pleasure, both heavenly and earthly, with the utmost constancy, leant on the bosom of her beloved with such great pressure and constant adherence that it seemed to her that the force of all creation would not be strong enough to shift her even a little from that resting-place where she was rejoicing to drink in, from the side of the Lord's body, life-giving savor, sweetness far surpassing balsam.

[3] 1 Pt 4:8

CHAPTER FIVE

THE LORD'S DESCENT TO HER WHEN SHE HAD CAST HERSELF DOWN

1. On the Feast of Saint Matthew the Apostle,[1] since the Lord had gone before her with a generous blessing of sweetness[2] at the elevation of the chalice, she was offering the same chalice to the Lord in thanksgiving. She began to reflect in her heart that she had done very little in offering that chalice, if she did not expose herself to endure sufferings for Christ's sake. Thus in an impulse of virtue she raised herself from the Lord's bosom, where she seemed to be taking great delight, and flung herself on the ground like a worthless corpse with these words: 'Lord, I expose myself to suffer all that could be a source of praise for you'.

At this the Lord immediately rose up in haste and lay down beside her on the ground. As if drawing her to him, he said, 'This is mine!' By virtue of his presence, reviving, she raised herself to the Lord and said, 'Yes, my Lord, I am the work of your hands'.[3] The Lord said, 'A new gift is yours: that my love for you is so tightly bound up with you that without you I cannot happily live'.

[1] 21 September.

[2] Ps 20:4.

[3] Response, *Laudabilis populus*, of Matins for Sundays in November.

In her astonishment at the great condescension of his words she said, 'Why do you say that, my Lord, when having deigned to take pleasure in your own creation you would have an unlimited number, both on earth and in heaven, with whom you could happily live, even if I had never been created?'

The Lord replied, 'He who has always lacked a limb is not tormented by the pain of one who had it cut off in adulthood; so I shall never, from the moment that I set my love upon you, suffer us to be separated from each other'.

CHAPTER SIX

HER SOUL WORKING WITH GOD

1. On Saint Maurice's day,[1] when Mass had been celebrated as far as the Secret when the host is consecrated, she said to the Lord: 'That work which you are now about to do, Lord, must be worthy of such priceless and surpassing honor that my wretched self dare not even look upon it. So, sinking out of sight, I shall throw myself into the deepest vale of humility that I can search out, awaiting there my share, for thence shall come forth salvation to all the chosen'.

The Lord replied: 'When a mother wants something embroidered to be worked in silk or pearls, sometimes she sets her little child in a higher place to hold her thread or her pearls for her, or to give her some sort of help. In the same way I have set you in a higher place to make you take part in this Mass. If you gladly applied your will to this labor, however difficult, you were willing to serve so that this offering may share its full effect in all Christians, living and dead, according to its dignity; then in your way you have helped me best in my work'.

[1] 22 September.

CHAPTER SEVEN

THE LORD'S COMPASSION

1. On Holy Innocents' day while she was being hampered by the turmoil of her thoughts in her preparation for communion, she was asking divine help on this. This was the answer she received from God's most courteous mercy: 'If anyone, attacked by human temptation, takes refuge with confident hope under my protection, he is one of those of whom I can say, "One is my dove,[1] as if chosen from thousands;[2] with a single glance of her eyes she has wounded my divine heart through and through",[3] so much so that, if I knew I could not help her, it would be such a source of sorrow to my heart that all the delights of heaven could not assuage it. For in my body which is united to my divinity, my chosen have always an advocate[4] who compels me to have compassion on their various needs'.

She replied, 'My Lord, how can your spotless body, in which you have never had any contradiction, compel you to have compassion on us in our anxieties that are so various?' To this the Lord replied, 'It is easy to persuade one who is understanding. For the apostle said of me, "He had to be made like his brethren in every

[1] Sg 6:8.

[2] Sg 5:10.

[3] Sg 4:9.

[4] 1 Jn 2:1.

respect, that he might become merciful'.[5] The Lord added, 'The "single glance" of my chosen one with which she had pierced my heart through and through is the sure trust that one ought to have in me, a trust that I truly have the power, the knowledge, and the will to be faithfully at her side in everything. This trust acts with such force on my loving-kindness that it is quite impossible for me to leave her'.

She said, 'My Lord, since trust is such a sure good, which no one can possess unless you have given it, how can someone who lacks it be at fault?' The Lord replied, 'Anyone at all can overcome his faintheartedness to a certain extent, at least on the evidence of Scripture. For he can say to me, if not with his whole heart at least with his mouth, that prayer of Job's: "Even if I have been plunged into the abyss of hell, you shall free me from there",[6] and that other prayer, "Even though you kill me, yet shall I trust in you" and others like it'.

[5]Heb 2:17.

[6]Former Response, glossing Jb 30:23–4, for 2 November.

CHAPTER EIGHT

THE DIVISION OF THE MASS INTO FIVE PARTS

1. One day when she was in bed and, unable to be present at Mass, was about to receive communion, she said to the Lord with troubled heart, 'Look, most loving, I can attribute the fact that I am prevented from being present at Mass today to your divine providence. How can I now prepare myself for receiving your most holy body and blood since, as it seems to me, the supreme preparation for me is always attention to the Mass?'

The Lord replied, 'Since you impute this motivation to me, pay attention to me and I shall sing you a sweet and loving nuptial song. Hear me say, then, that you are redeemed by my blood[1] and consider that the entire period of thirty-three years in which I toiled for you in this exile[2] had no other reason for its existence than as a preparatory mission for your betrothal. Let this serve for the first part of the Mass'.

'Hear me say that you are endowed with my spirit and learn that, just as for all those thirty-three years, as I have said, I toiled for you on that mission in body, so in spirit I celebrated our most

[1]Anthem for All Saints; cf. Rv 5:9.

[2]Cf. Bernard of Clairvaux, SC 11, 7.

delightful and longed-for nuptials that united you to me. Let this serve for the second part of the Mass'.

'Hear me also say that you are filled with my divinity and know that my divinity has the power, amid the outward troubles of the body, to provide inward spiritual delights that are most pleasant and acceptable. Let this serve as the third part of the Mass'.

'Hear me say further that you are made holy by my love, and recognize that your ability to please me comes entirely from me, not at all from yourself. Let this serve as the fourth part of the Mass'.

'Hear me say last of all that by my bonding you are exalted and know that since all power in heaven and earth has been given me[3] nothing can prevent me, if it so pleases me, raising you up with me for my good pleasure, just as it is appropriate for the woman who shares the king's bed to be called queen and as a result to be worthily honored. Delight in meditating on this, and from now on do not pretend that you had to go without Mass!'

[3]Mt 28:18.

CHAPTER NINE

THE DISPENSATION OF DIVINE GRACE

1. It had been divinely revealed to someone that the Lord would deign to release a great company of souls from the pains of Purgatory through the community's prayers. To gain this end a special prayer had been enjoined upon the whole community. Just like the others, the woman who is the subject of this book was completing the prayer enjoined upon her on the Sunday on which the company of souls already mentioned were to be released from their pains, and was offering herself to the Lord as devoutly as she could for the salvation of souls. Since she had drawn nearer the Lord and beheld him in his glory like a king bestowing rewards but could not clearly make out what the Lord seemed to be so busy about, she said to him: 'Most kindly Lord, last year on the feast of Saint Mary Magdalene you made known to me, unworthy as I am, that you were constrained by your own loving-kindness to lay all your kindliness at your feet because so many, by the example of that saint, a sinner but your true lover, had flung themselves in humility at your feet on that very day. Deign, too, in your mercy to make plain to the eyes of my understanding what you are doing now, for it is hidden from me'.

The Lord replied, 'I am distributing gifts'. By this she understood that the Lord was distributing the community's prayers for the healing of souls. However she could hardly see the souls themselves, even though they were there. Then the Lord added,

'Don't you too want to offer me the riches of your merit to add to what I have to give?'. She melted with pleasure at these words, not knowing that the entire community was doing this very thing at the suggestion of the person already mentioned to whom the promise had been made concerning the souls to be set free. She gratefully accepted what the Lord had requested, as if it were something he particularly wanted from her, and replied with cheerful heart, 'I offer you, Lord, not only my own spiritual possessions, which are worth next to nothing, but also those of the whole community from the common life which I share with them, claiming them as my own in their entirety, through your grace. This I do of my own free will, in the union of your perfection with great joy'. The Lord accepted this with great kindness.

2. Then the Lord, as if absorbed, stretched a cloud over himself and bent down to her alone and, tenderly raising her to him, said, 'Concentrate on me alone and enjoy the sweetness of my grace'. Then she said, 'Why, my sweetness, my God, do you deprive me so completely of that gift which you have so obviously bestowed on so-and-so—the gift of revelation of souls—when you kindly condescend to make plain to me so many of your secrets?' The Lord replied, 'Remember that you quite often vilify yourself because you think yourself so unworthy of the gift of my grace. You reckon this is bestowed on you as if on a hired laborer who is hired to serve and as if, without that gift, you could render me no fealty. For this reason you place others before yourself—others, who are hired with no such gift but none the less seem completely loyal to me. I have made you like them in that respect, so that you too, while you have no privileged knowledge concerning souls but still labor faithfully for them, may not be without that dignity that you extol in others'.

3. While he was speaking she realized, as if in a state of ecstasy, with what wonderful and inexpressible condescension the divine loving-kindness sometimes comes down to the human level, generously and copiously infusing its grace, and sometimes denies lesser gifts to protect humility, which is the foundation and the defense of graces. She also realized how the Lord causes both these to work together

for good[1] for the loving soul. And because of her great thankfulness and wonder at God's infinite goodness towards her, as if out of her mind and reduced to a state of collapse, she flung herself on the Lord's breast and said, 'My Lord, my insignificance cannot sustain this weight'. Then the Lord diminished the magnitude of that knowledge. When she regained her strength she said to the Lord, 'Because, most kindly Lord, the incomprehensible, unsearchable wisdom of your providence demands that I do without this gift, from now on I shall never desire further.'

4. She added: 'But surely, Lord, you hear me when I pray for certain of my friends?' As if confirming by an oath the Lord said, 'By my divine power, I do indeed'. She said, 'Therefore I now pray for that person who has been entrusted to me again and again'. At once she saw something like a little stream of crystalline purity come forth from the Lord's breast and flow into the innermost being of the person for whom she was praying. Then she asked the Lord, 'Lord, what use is this to that person, since she herself is not aware of this inflowing?' The Lord replied, 'When a doctor administers a medicinal potion to someone who is sick, it is not at the time that he drinks that potion that the bystanders see the invalid restored to health. Nor does the invalid himself feel immediately that he is cured. None the less the doctor who understands the power of the potion, knows very well how it should benefit the sick man'. She said, 'Why, Lord, do you not take from her her unruly temperament and the other failings, for which I have so often entreated you?' The Lord replied, 'It was said of me as the child Jesus, "He grew in years and in wisdom, in the sight of God and of men".[2] So let that person, who is growing from one hour to the next, create virtue from vice; I shall take from her all that is human so that after this life she may behold all that I have prepared for the human being whom I have arranged to raise above the angels'.

5. As the time drew near at which she was to receive communion, she besought the Lord that he would deign to advance the time

[1]Rom 8:28.
[2]Lk 2:52.

of his grace for as many sinners (who were none the less destined to be saved, for she did not presume to pray for the damned) as there were souls, released from the pains of purgatory through the prayers of that person who has been mentioned repeatedly, that had on that very day joined the choirs of heaven. The Lord corrected her faintheartedness and said, 'Does not the high worth of the presence of my immaculate body and precious blood deserve that even those who are in a state of damnation should be called to a state of better living?' Pondering his generous liberality in these words she said, 'Since your inestimable loving-kindness deigns to descend to my unworthy prayers, I pray your majesty, in union with the love and longing of all your creation, to grant me as many souls of living sinners, who are currently in a state of damnation, as the number of souls you have already granted me, so that they for whom you prayed with greatest condescension may come to your grace, at whatever time and in whatever place it may be. Nor do I choose any of my friends, relations or kinsfolk'. The Lord kindly accepted this suggestion and assured her this would be so.

6. Then she said, 'I would like to know, Lord, what you wish me to add to these prayers'. Receiving no reply she said, 'Lord, I suppose that my unfaithfulness does not deserve to receive an answer to these questions, for you, who know every heart,[3] realize that I am so negligent that I would quite likely not carry out anything you enjoined on me'. Then the Lord with a serene countenance replied lovingly, 'Trust alone can most easily obtain all things; but if your devotion does not shrink from something extra, recite the psalm "Praise the Lord all ye peoples"[4] three hundred and sixty-five times, to make up the measure of my divine praise, which has been slighted by those very souls'.

[3]Est 13:12, Dn 13:42, Jn 21:17.

[4]Ps 116:1.

CHAPTER TEN

THREE OFFERINGS

1. On the feast of Saint Matthias,[1] since she had made up her mind not to receive communion because she was hampered for many reasons, during the first mass she was concentrating on God and herself. The Lord showed himself to her with as strong an emotion of friendship as ever friend could render friend with tender emotion. She however was not at all satisfied by this, for she was accustomed to more potent favors bestowed in more potent fashion. She longed to be completely ravished from her own being and to be given over to her beloved who is called a consuming fire[2] and, melted by the fire of that very charity, to become one with that love in an intimate bonding.

And since she could not work for this at that time, turning away to God's praise she returned to another form of devotion to which she was accustomed, rendering high praise. That is, she extolled the vast bounty and condescension of the all-worshipful Trinity, first for every grace that has ever flowed from its profound overabundance to the benefit of all the saints; second, for every grace granted to the most worthy Mother; third, for every grace poured into the most holy humanity of Jesus Christ. She prayed to all [the saints], as a

1 14 May
2 Heb 12:29.

group, and to each individually, that each one of them might bring as a sacrifice to the radiant and ever-peaceful Trinity, to make up for her own sins of omission, all that devotion and preparedness with which, on the day of their own assumptions, they had stood before the sight of the Lord's glory in a state of perfection to receive their eternal reward. This she did by reciting three times 'Praise the Lord, all ye peoples'[3] and so on—first for All Saints, second for the blessed Virgin, third for the Son of God. At this the Lord said, 'How are you to reward my saints who make such an offering on your behalf, since you intend to omit that offering [i.e. communion] that you are accustomed to make in thanksgiving on their behalf?' At this she became silent.

2. Then at the offering of the host with a great desire she desired[4] to find an offering that she could worthily offer God the Father to his eternal praise. This was the reply she received from the Lord to this request: 'If you were to fit yourself today to receive the sacrament of my life-giving body and blood, you could most certainly obtain that threefold blessing for which you prayed at this Mass: that is, to enjoy my most loving sweetness and, melted by the fire of my godhead, to flow into me just as gold is fused with silver. From this you would have a most precious alloy which you could most worthily offer God the Father to his eternal praise, and all the saints would have most fully their complete reward'.

Overcome by these words she was inflamed by so great a desire that it would not have seemed hard to her to fly to the most saving sacrament even through the midst of swords. When she was devoutly thanking God after she had received the Lord's body, the lover of men and women[5] himself spoke to her as follows: 'Today by your own will you decided to serve me with the others with straw, mortar and brick;[6] but I chose you to be among those who would most sweetly take their fill of the delicacies of my royal table.'

[3]Ps 116; cf. Chapter 9.

[4]Lk 22:15.

[5]From the sequence *Mittit ad Virginem*.

[6]Ex 1:14.

And when on the same day another person had refrained from holy communion for no good reason, she said to the Lord, 'Why, most merciful Lord, did you allow her to be tempted in this way?' The Lord replied, 'Is it my fault that she has pulled the veil of her unworthiness over her eyes for so long that she was completely unable to discern the loving-kindness of my fatherly affection?'

CHAPTER ELEVEN

AN INDULGENCE, AND HER DESIRE FOR THE DIVINE WILL

1. Hearing one day an indulgence of very many years being preached that could be gained for almsgiving, she said to the Lord with devout heart: 'Lord, if I were at this moment endowed with great riches, I would most willingly offer vast quantities of gold and silver,[1] so that I might be absolved from my sins through that indulgence, to the honor and glory of your name'.

The Lord kindly replied, 'Then by the authority of my divine nature, accept full remission for all your sins and omissions'. Immediately she saw her soul shining in snowy brightness, free from every spot. Then, after some days, when she came to herself and found her soul still shining with the same brightness that she had known before, she began to fear that she was deceived in such a display of her soul's innocence. For she thought that certainly the purity which had earlier been revealed, even if it had been genuine, none the less seemed somewhat clouded as result of her continual lapses into omissions and frivolity which she had quite often committed from human weakness. The Lord kindly comforted her sense of desolation with these words: 'Do I not keep for myself a greater

[1]Ezr 8:30.

power than I have conferred on my creatures? For I have endowed the material sun with such power that, if a white cloth has become stained, the stain suddenly vanishes as a result of the power of the sun's heat and intensity and the cloth is restored to an even brighter whiteness than before. How much more will I be able to preserve a soul at which I, the sun's creator, have directed the glance of my mercy, undefiled from every speck of sin or omission? For I purify every stain in it by the force of my white-hot love'.

2. Then another time she grew so weak from meditating on her unworthiness and faintheartedness that she was quite incapable of exerting herself in God's praise or of panting after the enjoyment of contemplation in her usual manner. At length, by the Lord's freely-given mercy, through communion with the most holy conversation of Christ Jesus, she was so moved that, it seemed to her, she went forward in accordance with her desire and stood before the lord, the king of kings,[2] in that beauty in which Esther, it is thought, stood before King Ahasuerus.[3] The kindly grace of the savior spoke to her with these words: 'What is your command, lady queen?' She replied, 'I beseech you, Lord, and desire with all my heart that your most praiseworthy will may be accomplished in me according to your best good pleasure'.[4] Then the Lord, enumerating one by one all those people who had entrusted themselves to her prayers, said, 'What then do you ask for her, for her, and for her, who have specially entrusted themselves to your prayers today?' She replied, 'All I wish to ask on their behalf, Lord, is that your most gentle will may be accomplished in all those people'. After this the Lord spoke again: 'What do you want me to do for you?' She replied, 'It is my earnest wish, taking precedence over every delight, that your most gentle, most praiseworthy will may be accomplished in me as in all creation. And to accomplish this may I be found most ready to expose any part of my body to any suffering whatsoever.' To these words the most benign loving-kindness of God, which had gone

[2]Cf. Rv 17:14 and 19:16.

[3]Est 2:12.

[4]Cf. Eph 1:9.

before her in longing and rewarded her in following after,[5] replied: 'Because you have been zealous in furthering my will with such great loving devotion, according to my customary benevolence I reward your effort with this gift: that you may appear as pleasing in my eyes as if you had never in the least disregarded my will'.

[5]From the prayer *Actiones nostras*.

CHAPTER TWELVE

THE TRANSFIGURATION EFFECTED BY GRACE

1. While the antiphon 'On my bed'[1] was being sung, including the phrase that is repeated four times in that antiphon, that is, 'whom my soul loves', she understood that there are, as it were, four ways in which God may be sought by the faithful soul. By the first, that is, 'On my bed through the night I have sought him whom my soul loves', she understood the first route by which God is sought, on the bed of contemplation through the extolling of praise. Then follows, 'I have sought him and have not found him', for the soul, enveloped by mortal flesh,[2] can never be fully expanded in the praise of God.

By the second verse that follows, 'I will rise up and go about the city, through the streets and the squares, seeking him whom my soul loves',[3] she understood zeal for thanksgiving, by which the soul considers thoroughly[4] 'through the streets and the squares,' that is, the various ways in which God does good to his creation. Hence

[1] Sg 3:1.

[2] From the Ritual for the consecration of virgins.

[3] Sg 3:2.

[4] Cf. Jb 5:27.

there follows in this place, because here too she was totally unable to render suitable praise, 'I have sought him and not found him'.

By the third verse that follows, 'The sentinels who guard the city found me', she understood God's justice and mercy, by which the recollected soul comes to herself, and considering her own unworthiness in the light of God's blessings, begins to seek the Lord's mercy through lamenting and repenting her own evil deeds, while she says: 'Surely you have seen him whom my soul loves?'[5]

In this way, distrustful of her own merits, she turned in humble trust to the divine loving-kindness through devout prayer and sometimes through the inspiration of grace she found him whom the faithful soul loves.

2. When the antiphon was over, as a result of this and other things (which it would be impossible to commit to writing) which the divine loving-kindness granted her the grace of perceiving through this antiphon, she was aware that her heart was moved by such a powerful force that every limb was so moved that she seemed to have lost the use of all her limbs. She then said to the Lord, 'Now it seems to me I can truly say: "Behold, my beloved, not only my inward parts but all my limbs are moved on your account" '.[6] The Lord replied, 'I best perceive and know what flows from me and flows back into me. But you, still enveloped by mortal flesh, will never be able to know how, in return, all the sweetness of my high worth is moved on your account'. And he added: 'Know this, however, that from the movement of this grace you have achieved a splendor in my sight such as that which my body received on Mount Tabor before my three disciples. And so I too, moved by the sweetness of charity, may fitly say of you: "This is my beloved son, in whom I am well pleased".[7] For it is always the proper accompaniment of such grace that through its workings both body and soul are miraculously illuminated with brilliant shining splendor'.

[5] Sg 3:3.

[6] Gn 43:30.

[7] Mt 17:5.

CHAPTER THIRTEEN

THE HIGHEST FORM OF REPARATION

1. One day it happened that a host fell out of the altar-hanging while it was being folded, and there was some doubt as to whether or not it had been consecrated. When she was seeking the Lord's advice on this, and having learnt from him, understood that the host had not been consecrated, she was overjoyed, quite rightly, because such negligence had not been perpetrated. In her eagerness for the gain of God's praise, however, she said to the Lord: 'Although your immense loving-kindness forestalled here the exhibition of such an affront towards you in the sacrament of the altar, nevertheless, since you, Lord of all, have so often undeservedly suffered similar affronts, not only from your enemies—that is, pagans and Jews—but also, alas, from your dearest friends—that is, the faithful redeemed by your precious blood and, I weep to say it,[1] even on occasions, by priests and religious—I shall never reveal that this host was not consecrated, lest you should be cheated through me of some reparation'.

2. She went on, 'Grant, Lord God, that I may understand what reparation would be most acceptable for any offense. For even if I have to deploy all my strength, I will be eager and willing to carry it out for the praise and glory of your love'. Then she

[1] Phil 3:18.

understood that the Lord would accept it if in honor of his most holy members she were to recite two hundred and twenty-five Our Fathers, and if the same number of works of charity were shown towards her neighbors, in reverence for him who said: 'Whatever you have done to one of the least of mine, you have done for me',[2] in union with that love through which God became man for our sakes. He would also accept the same number of rejections of vain and unprofitable pleasures, offered for his divine pleasure. How great, how unspeakable is the mercy and loving-kindness of the Lord our lover, who accepts such gifts so greatly from us, and even rewards offerings which, if they were not to be offered, a suitable and painful vengeance would rightly follow!

[2]Mt 25:40.

CHAPTER FOURTEEN

TWO FORMS OF REPARATION

1. The Lord is everywhere so eager for the salvation of his chosen ones that it is sometimes his custom to burden them so much with ordinary things that an extraordinary accumulation of merits accrues to them from then on. So on one occasion he made the confession she was about to make so burdensome that it seemed to her that she was quite incapable of carrying it out by her own efforts. So with what devotion she could, she commended herself to the Lord in prayer. And for this she received the following reply from him: 'Do you entrust this confession to me with such complete confidence that you will expend no further effort to carry it out?' She answered, 'Yes. I have complete—and more than complete—trust in your omnipotence and kindliness, my most loving Lord. But I think it wrong to inflict injury on you with my sins unless, taking the pains to ponder them in the bitterness of my soul, I shall have shown you that I intend to make some reparation'. When the Lord gladly accepted these words and she had completely devoted herself to recalling her own sins, she saw herself with her skin somewhat torn, as if she had been rolling in thorny stubble. When she was exposing this wretched condition of hers for healing to the Father of mercies,[1] as a most experienced and trustworthy physician, he

[1]2 Cor 1:3.

kindly bent down and said to her: 'With my divine breath I shall heat up for you the bath of confession. When you have been washed in it as you please, you will stand before me spotless'. Longing to strip herself for this bath she said to the Lord, 'So far, my lord, do I lay aside all human favor for love of your splendor that you would find me ready even if I had to publish all my wrong-doings to the whole world'. Then, as if she were naked, the Lord covered her with his own garment and holding her to his bosom made her wait until after the bath was ready.

2. As the time of confession came nearer, while she was much burdened by inner conflicts, she said to the Lord, 'Since the loving Heart of your fatherly mercy knows very well how hard it is for me to make this confession, why do you permit me, kindly God, to be burdened even more by inner conflicts?' The Lord replied, "Girls who are bathing are usually helped by the hands of those who rub them down; so you are advanced by the annoyance of inner conflicts.' Then, as there was being displayed on the Lord's left a bath, as it were, giving off great heat, the Lord also showed her on his right a certain garden of the most charming delights, in bloom with all kinds of flowers. But more especially there appeared in this garden the most beautiful roses without thorns, which exuded a life-giving sweetness in the fresh vitality of their vigorous flowering and by their marvelous attractions they drew those who came near. He indicated that she might enter this charming garden, if she preferred it to the bath which she pleaded was too hot for her. To this she replied, 'By no means, Lord! I shall unhesitatingly enter the bath which you have heated for me with your divine breath'. And the Lord said, 'May this be your eternal salvation'.

3. She understood therefore that the aforesaid garden signified the inner sweetness of divine grace which, when the gentle south wind of love is pleasantly blowing,[2] rains down the nectar-dew of loving tears on the faithful soul and suddenly makes her whiter than snow[3] and completely sure not only of forgiveness of her sins but also of

[2]Sg 4:16.

[3]Cf. Ps 50:9.

the accumulation of superabundant merits. From this she knew that it was most welcome to the Lord that because of his love she should choose the more burdensome task, leaving the more pleasant. And when she had, after confession, entered her place of prayer, she was aware that the Lord of his great courtesy was there. Yet by his order that confession became a burden to her, so much so that she labored with the greatest difficulty in mentioning those things which some people, as if boasting, do not blush to proclaim before everyone.

4. It should also be known that the soul is purified from all sin[4] in two ways in particular. In the first, that is, through the bitterness of penitence and all that goes with it, denoted by the bath; in the second way, through the delightful conflagration of divine love and all that goes with it, signified by the charming garden. After confession in fact she was fixed in contemplation of the wound of the Lord's left hand, as if she were resting in exhaustion after a bath, until she had satisfied the penance laid upon her by the priest. But since this penance was of such a nature that it had to be postponed for a while, she was very concerned whether, before its satisfaction, she might not be granted more intimate and free access to her sweetest and most loving Lord. And so during Mass, when the most sacred host was being offered by the priest as the surest, most efficacious reconciliation for the fault of all humanity, she offered it to the Lord in thanksgiving for the blessing of the bath and in acceptable reparation for all her faults. When this had been accepted, she too was accepted into the bosom of the most kindly Father and she there felt that the day-spring from on high had truly visited her in the inmost parts of his mercy[5] and truth.

[4] 2 Cor 7:1.

[5] Lk 1:78; cf. the canticle *Benedictus.*

CHAPTER FIFTEEN

THE TREE OF LOVE

1. On the next day during Mass, at the moment of the elevation of the host, as if half-asleep she was not paying much attention to her devotion. But at the sound of the sanctuary-bell, she suddenly as it were woke up and saw the King the Lord[1] Jesus, holding with both his hands a tree which was, as it were, cut off near the ground but laden with the most beautiful fruit and from every single leaf giving out rays like a star of marvelous brightness. And when he shook this tree in the court of heaven, he rejoiced marvelously in its fruit. Indeed, after a little while the Lord put down that tree in the midst of the garden of her heart, that she might strive to increase its fruit, and she might rest beneath it and thereby be refreshed. While she had returned to her self and was undertaking this task, she soon began, in the increase of fruits, to pray for a certain person who had annoyed her very recently, suggesting that she should choose to undergo yet again the bitter sorrow which she had just experienced so that the grace of God should be given more generously to the one who was troubling her. Meanwhile she suddenly recalled to mind on the top of the tree a flower of the most lovely color, which was about to bear fruit if she brought her good will into effect. For by that tree was symbolized charity, which abounds not only in the

[1] Is 6:5.

fruit of good works but also in the flowers of good will, and even in the shining leaves of sweet effect. From this the citizens of heaven take extraordinary delight, when one human being condescends to another and strives to alleviate the needs of neighbors, as far as possible. At the very moment of the elevation of the host, she received wonderful adornment of gilded clothing[2] over the rosy pink[3] she had received the day before when she reclined on the breast of the Lord.

2. The same day, during None, the Lord appeared in the guise of a blooming, delightful young man, asking her to offer him nuts,[4] gathering them from that aforementioned tree. To do this he lifted her up and placed her on a branch of the tree. At this she said, 'Sweetest youth, why do you ask this of me, who am as weak in strength as in gender, when it would be more suitable for you to offer them to me?' 'Not so', he said. 'The bride who is, as it were, at home in her own house with her parents can act with greater confidence than the bashful bridegroom, who for the sake of visiting only sometimes turns aside to her. But if the bride is at all considerate towards the groom's bashfulness, when he takes her into his own house he will promptly pay her dear recompense for everything'.

By this means he let her understand how unreasonable is that excuse by which some people say, 'If God wanted me to do this or that, he would certainly give me the grace for it', since it is quite right that in this life a person should, as it were, crush her own opinion for God's sake and not consent to her own will in anything that concerns her own convenience. And in the future this will be most gratefully rewarded.

Since she wanted to offer him the nuts, the young man climbed up to her. He sat down, told her to crack the nuts, extract the kernel and prepare them for him to eat. He let her understand by this means that it is not enough for a person to crush their own opinion so as to benefit an enemy, unless they themselves also search out an

[2] Ps 44:10/45:9.

[3] Presumably the 'garment' mentioned in Chapter 14.1.

[4] Cf. Sg 6:10.

opportunity to put it into effect. For the purpose of all this was to indicate by these nuts that, namely, one should do good to those who persecute one. And so the Lord showed her nuts, which have a bitter, hard shell, growing on the same tree as apples! For the love of one's enemies ought to be mingled with the sweetness of God's savor, by which anyone may be prepared to suffer death for Christ's sake.

CHAPTER SIXTEEN

THE PROFIT OF DESOLATION; SPIRITUAL COMMUNICATION

1. While the community was chanting the Mass 'Hail, holy Mother', in honor of the Mother of God, on the last day before the divine rites were to be suspended,[1] amid the words of prayer she spoke to the Lord: 'How will you console us, most kindly God, for our present trouble?' The Lord answered, 'I shall increase my delights among you. Just as a husband enjoys his wife more freely in private than in public, so your sighs and desolations shall be my delights. Indeed among you progress in my love shall increase, just as hidden fire spreads more widely. Moreover, just as rising water suddenly overflows with a rush, so shall my delights in you and your love in me overflow, to the increase of both'.

Then she asked, 'And how long will this interdict last?' The Lord replied, 'As long as it lasts those favors will last'. She rejoined, 'It would seem shameful to great princes if one of the lowest of the low, of utter worthlessness, were admitted to their confidences. In the same way it could seem inappropriate to you, the King of kings, if the secrets of your divine providence were revealed to

[1]The community at Helfta was placed under an interdict, because of litigation concerning a debt, a little before AD 1296.

me, the dregs of all your creation.[2] I believe that is why I have not been given an assurance, even though the end of all things is known to you before their beginning'. The Lord replied, 'Not at all; but it is out of the grand design for your salvation; for although I raise you up through contemplation, sometimes admitting you to my confidence, I also sometimes shut you out to safeguard your humility, so that when you do receive it you may discover what you are thanks to me, and when you are again deprived you may realize what you are in yourself'.

2. During the offertory, that is: 'Remember, Virgin Mother', at these words: 'that you may ask good things for us', while she was concentrating on the Mother of every grace the Lord intervened, saying, 'It is not necessary for anyone to ask for you,[3] as I for my own part am entirely pleased with you'.[4] But she, remembering numerous failings, both her own and those of certain other women, and being unsure how the Lord could assert that he was 'entirely pleased', understood the Lord was gently saying, 'My natural goodness influences me so that I see the better side, which I embrace with my entire divine nature, raising up what is less perfect to what is more perfect'. Then she said, 'Generous giver, how can you impart to me, so unworthy and unprepared, the gifts of your grace that are now so great and so full of consolation?' The Lord replied, 'Love compelled me'. She said, 'Where now are those stains which I contracted as a result of my heart's impatience, into which I fell a little earlier and made rather obvious in my words?' To this the Lord said, 'The fire of my divine nature has completely consumed them, for in any soul on which I rest in my grace and favor I consume every ugly stain'. Then she said, 'Most merciful God, as long as your grace so often forestalls my unworthiness, I would like to know if such faults as the impatience I mentioned and others like it will have to be purified in my soul after my death?' When the Lord kindly failed to answer, she added, 'Truly, Lord, if the beauty of your

[2] 1 Cor 4:13.

[3] *vos*, i.e. '[all of] you'.

[4] Cf. Lk 3:22.

justice[5] demands it, I would freely and willingly go down even into hell that I might by this means more worthily make reparation to you. But if it greatly exalts your natural goodness and mercy that all things should be consumed by your love, with complete frankness I shall demand that your love should purify every stain of my soul, far beyond what is deserved!' The Lord, in accordance with the fullness of his divine nature and loving-kindness, kindly granted this.

3. On the next day while Mass was being celebrated for the local people,[6] at the time of communion she said to the Lord, 'Do you not pity us, most merciful Father, in that now, because of those goods by which we ought to be sustained in your service, we are deprived of the precious good of your body and blood?' The Lord replied, 'How could I feel great pity if, when I am leading my bride towards flowery and charming places of refreshment, turning aside to some more barren place before we arrive, I would with my own hand straighten out some disorder in her clothes or finery, so that I might lead her in the more fitly?' Then she said, 'My Lord, how can those people who have imposed this burden on us possess your grace?' The Lord said, 'Let it be. I shall deal with them in this matter'.

4. Then, about the time of the offering of the saving victim, when she was offering that same host to the Lord for his eternal praise and for the salvation of the whole convent, the Lord, taking that host into himself and breathing forth life-giving delight from his inmost being, said, 'From this breath I shall feed them with divine nourishment'. Then she said to the Lord, 'Surely you will not now give communion to the whole community?' He replied, 'No, only to those who desire it, and those who would like to desire it. But the others, since they belong to the convent, shall have such great profit that a strong desire shall yet be given them, like someone who has little interest in food but, when attracted for some time by its pleasant smell, begins to take pleasure in eating it'.

[5]Jer 50:7.

[6]Apparently only the nuns themselves were affected by the interdict.

5. On the day of the Assumption when at the elevation of the host she understood that the Lord was saying, 'I come that I may sacrifice myself to God the Father on behalf of my members', she replied, 'My most loving Lord, surely you are not allowing us, your members, to be cut off from you by this curse of excommunication with which those who are trying to take away our goods are threatening us?' The Lord replied, 'If someone is capable of understanding the quintessence of my inmost being, by which you cleave to me, let him cut you off from me'. And the Lord added, 'The curse of excommunication imposed on you for that reason will do you no more harm than an attempt to cut something with a little wooden knife, which is quite unable to penetrate but just leaves a slight knife-mark'. Then she said to the Lord, 'Lord God, since you who are infallible truth have intimated to me, though quite unworthy, that you have decided to increase your delights in us and add to our love for you, how then is it that some women are claiming that they have grown very cool in their love for you?' The Lord replied, 'I contain every good thing in myself and to each at the ordained time I give a part suited to the individual'.

CHAPTER SEVENTEEN

THE LORD'S CONDESCENSION AND SHARING OF GRACE

1. On one Sunday which coincided with the feast of Saint Laurence,[1] and also with the commemoration of the dedication of the chapel, during the first Mass she was praying for certain women who had devoutly entrusted themselves to her prayers. She saw come forth from the throne of heaven to earth a branch of a green vine; by the shoots of its leaves an ascent was provided from the bottom to the top. She understood that this ascent was faith, by which the chosen rise up to heavenly things. And then she recognized that in its heights, as if at the left-hand of the throne, very many members of the community were there and the Son of God, as if in the presence of the heavenly Father, was standing with proper reverence at the moment that the convent would have been about to receive communion, if the interdict had not prevented it. She greatly desired that the life-giving sacrament should be offered spiritually both to herself and to the others present, out of the divine mercy which no human power can withstand. Then she saw the Lord Jesus dip the host which he held in his hand as it were in the heart of God the Father and bring it out tinted a rosy red, as if reddened by blood. In great doubt at this, she pondered in her heart what this

[1] 10 August.

meant, since red denotes suffering and God the Father could never be reddened by any mark of suffering. While she was brooding on this, she failed to notice that she was experiencing the effect of her aforementioned desire, except that after a while she understood that the Lord had accomplished a respite of repose for himself in the hearts and souls of every one of those women whom earlier she had recognized raised on high. How this had happened, however, she could not know.

2. Meanwhile, mindful of someone who had entrusted herself humbly and devoutly to her prayers just before Mass, she prayed for her, that the Lord might make her partaker[2] in this honor just described. To this she received the following reply: 'No one can come so far along the ascent of faith shown you unless raised up through trust, which that woman for whom you are now praying does not have'. She replied, 'Lord, it seems to me that humility, to which you customarily infuse more abundant grace, lessens her trust'. The Lord replied, 'I shall come down and impart my gifts both to her and to others settled in the valley [of humility]'.

Next the Lord of hosts[3] was seen to come down as if by a red ladder and after a while appeared in the midst of the chapel altar robed in pontifical vestments, holding in his hands a pyx like those in which the consecrated Host is usually kept. And throughout the whole Mass he remained seated, facing the priest, until the Preface. So great a crowd of angels were in his service that all the chapel on the Lord's right (that is, the north end) seemed full. They were displaying a particular joy because they were encompassing with great affection those places where devout prayers had frequently been offered by their fellow-citizens, that is, the community. On the Lord's left (that is, towards the south) stood just one choir of angels; a choir of apostles and separate choirs of martyrs, confessors and virgins joined them. When she perceived this and recollected in astonishment that incorruption, according to the Scriptures, brings one near to God,[4] she understood that between the Lord and the

[2]Cf. 1 Cor. 9:23.

[3]Cf. Ps. 23:10 etc.

[4]Ws 6:20.

blessed virgins was shining a special splendor of snowy whiteness, which united the virgins to the Lord more than the other saints, with a most delightful caress and intimacy of astonishing joy. She also understood that some rays of extraordinary brightness were stretched out to members of the community as if there were no obstacle between them and the Lord, although many solid walls separated them from the chapel in which he was seen.

3. And while she was taking extraordinary pleasure in this, concerned for other members too of the community she said to the Lord, 'Since your generous loving-kindness, Lord, has now given me the graces of such incredible sweetness, what do you give to those men who, perhaps at this very moment sweating at external activities, do not enjoy similar graces?' The Lord replied, 'I anoint them with balsam, even though they are, as it were, drowsy'. When she weighed up its power she was greatly astonished at how those who made an effort in the spiritual life and those who did not could possess so equal a reward: for balsam renders incorruptible those bodies anointed with it and it makes very little difference whether those anointed are asleep or awake! She also received this more comprehensible analogy as an example: that is, that when a person eats, by which the whole body is strengthened in every individual member, nevertheless only the mouth delights in the taste of the food. In the same way, when a special grace is granted to those who have been chosen, out of God's unrestrained loving-kindness merit also increases for all members [of the Church] and especially for those belonging to the same community, with the exception of those who deprive themselves of it through envy and ill-will.

4. In the meantime while 'Glory to God in the highest' was being intoned, the Lord Jesus our great high priest sent a divine breath like a burning flame towards heaven, to the glory of the Father. And at the words 'and on earth peace to men of good will' he sent forth the same breath, in the guise of snowy splendor, towards those present. Next, at 'Lift up your hearts', the Son of God arose and, as if through his powerful magnetism, drew to himself the desires of all those present. Then turning towards the east, pavilioned about on every side with a phalanx of countless angels, he stood with raised

hands and offered up the prayers of the faithful in the words of the Preface to God the Father. After this, while they began the 'Lamb of God', the Lord raised himself on the altar with all his power and at the second 'Lamb of God' flowed with his unsearchable wisdom into the inmost depths of every single person there. And at the third 'Lamb of God', collecting himself on high, he presented the prayers and desires of all in his self-offering to God the Father. Thus, out of the abundance of sweetness he granted with his own blessed mouth the kiss of peace to all the saints present, offering this privilege before others to the company of virgins, so that after the kiss of the mouth he also planted an intensely sweet kiss on their breast. And after this the Lord offered himself, as if completely overflowing with the honey-sweet love of divinity, to the community, saying, 'I am wholly yours. Then enjoy me, all of you according to your desire'. After this she said to the Lord, 'Lord, though I am now replete with inconceivable sweetness, nevertheless when you sit on the altar you seem to be further away from me. Thence through the blessing of this mass bring it about in me that my soul may feel united to you'. This the Lord carried out in such a way that through the Lord's embraces she felt herself pressed to his breast, with as much pleasure as potency, in divine union.

CHAPTER EIGHTEEN

THE GIFT OF PREPAREDNESS TO RECEIVE THE BODY OF CHRIST, AND MANY OTHER POINTS BESTOWED AT THAT SAME TIME

1. One day when she was coming forward to receive the life-giving sacrament, while the phrase 'Holy, holy, holy' in the antiphon 'Rejoice and be glad' was being sung, she fell to the ground in humility of heart and prayed the Lord that he would condescend to prepare her so that she might participate worthily in the heavenly banquets, to his praise and the profit of the whole world. The Son of God, like a sweet lover, quickly leant towards her and imprinted a most delightful kiss on her soul while the second 'Holy' was being sung: 'Behold, in this kiss, with that "Holy" which is addressed to me, I give you all the holiness of my divine and human natures, so that you may come to communion worthily prepared by it'.

2. On the Sunday following, while she was thanking God for that gift, there was the Son of God, more beautiful in form[1] than thousands of angels, taking her[2] up in his arms as if he were glorying

[1]Ps 44:3.

[2]Reading *suscipiens* rather than *suspiciens*.

in her. He joyfully presented her to God the Father in the perfection of that holiness which he had given her in his own name.[3] Then God the Father too, through his Only-begotten, took such pleasure with her in her soul that, as if unable to contain himself, he too with the Holy Spirit bestowed upon her their own 'Holy', so that she might gain the full blessing of complete holiness, both that of the Almighty, of Wisdom, and of Goodness.

3. Another time, when she was about to receive communion, she saw that very many women were prevented from communion for various reasons. Rejoicing in spirit, she said to the Lord out of the deepest affection of her heart,[4] 'I give you thanks, my God and most beloved lover, because you have brought me to such a condition that neither my relatives nor any other reasons can prevent me from sharing in your most joyful feast'. The Lord, according to the usual sweetness of his goodness, replied, 'Just as you declare that there is nothing to prevent you, so you should know that absolutely nothing, in heaven or on earth, or rather neither judgment nor justice is strong enough to prevent me from blessing you according to the high pleasure of my divine Heart'.

4. Similarly, another time when she was approaching communion while she greatly desired to be worthily prepared by the Lord, the sweet and loving Lord caressed her with these words:[5] 'Look, I am now donning you like a garment so that I can stretch out my tender hand unharmed among rough sinners, to bless them. Also I am clothing you with myself so that you may draw all those whom you bring before my presence in your mindfulness, or rather all those who are like you in nature, to that honor so that I can bless them in accordance with my royal generosity'.

5. On another day when she was about to take part in the divine mysteries, while she was recalling God's blessings towards her, that verse from the Book of Kings came into her mind: 'Who am I, or

[3] *ex persona sua.*

[4] RB 7.51.

[5] Est 15:11.

what is the house of my father?'[6] She rejected that phrase, 'what is the house of my father?', as if those had been people who in their day had lived according to God's ordinance, and thought of herself as a little offshoot which, receiving blessings from the proximity of the unquenchable fire of the Divine Heart, naturally catching fire in herself but growing steadily weaker as from carelessness because of her faults of negligence, and now as if reduced to nothing,[7] was lying there like a tiny burnt-out coal. When she turned to the most kindly intercessor Jesus, Son of God, praying that he would deign to present her, such as she was, to be reconciled to God the Father, Jesus himself, most loving, through the warm breath of the love of his wounded Heart, seemed to draw her to himself and wash her in the water flowing from it, then flood her in the life-giving blood of his Heart. At this she grew in strength from a minuscule coal to a vigorous green tree[8] whose branches were divided into three, like those of a lily. The Son of God took the tree and presented it with gratitude and glory to the Trinity that must always be adored. When it was presented, the wholly blessed Trinity inclined towards her with such great regard that God the Father, out of his divine omnipotence, hung on its upper branches every fruit which that soul could have produced if she had conformed as she should to divine omnipotence. Similarly the Son of God and the Holy Spirit seemed to hang the fruits of wisdom and goodness on the other two branches.

6. After this, when she had received the body of Christ, she saw that her soul, in the likeness of a tree as has been said above, had its root fixed in the wounded side of Jesus Christ. Through that wound, as if through a root, she felt in a new and wonderful way as if she were penetrated by the power of the divine and human natures together through each branch, fruit and leaf simultaneously. As a result the fruit of all his way of life on earth gained a new splendor through her, as gold shines through crystal. Thence not only the blessed

[6]1 Sm 18:18.

[7]Jb 30:15.

[8]Cf. Lk 13:19.

Trinity but also all the saints received the delight of a wonderful joy. In honor of the tree all rose up[9] and as it were bent the knee, one by one they offered their own merits in the shape of crowns, hanging them on the branches of that tree, to the praise and glory of him who, shining through it with new delight, deigned that they should feel joy.

But when she prayed the Lord that at least he would now give to all those in heaven, on earth and in purgatory (who would all by right have had the benefit from the fruit of her works if she had not neglected them) the benefit of the fruits bestowed on her by the divine goodness, each kind in which the fruit of the tree appeared began to exude a most potent liquor. Part, flowing onto those in heaven, piled up their joy; part, flowing into purgatory, lessened their pains; part, flowing to the earth, increased sweetness of grace for the righteous and bitterness of penitence for sinners.

7. One day during Mass at the elevation of the host, while she was offering that most sacred host to God the Father as worthy reparation for all sinners and as compensation for all her own acts of neglect, she perceived that her soul was brought before the gaze of the divine majesty in that good pleasure[10] in which Christ Jesus, splendor and image of the glory of his Father,[11] Lamb of God without spot, offered himself at the same time on the altar to God the Father for the salvation of the world. For God the Father saw her through the most blameless human nature of Jesus Christ as purified from all sin and spotless, and saw her through his most excellent divine nature as enriched and adorned with every sort of virtue with which that glorious divine nature flowered through his most holy human nature.

8. While to the best of her ability she was thanking the Lord, delighting in such wonderful regard of the divine loving-kindness, she gained this insight from him: as often as someone attends Mass with devotion, concentrating on God who there offers himself in

[9]Cf. RB 9.7.

[10]Eph 1:9.

[11]Col 1:15, Heb 1:3; prayer over the gifts at Mass.

the sacrament for the common salvation of the whole world, he is truly seen by God the Father as with the same good pleasure as God looks on the sacred host that is offered to him. It is like someone who steps from darkness into the radiance of the sunlight and is at once completely flooded with light. Then she asked the Lord, 'My Lord, does someone who falls into sin immediately lose this blessedness, just as someone who retreats from the light of the sun into the dark loses the welcome brightness of light?' The Lord replied, 'No; for although in sinning to a certain extent he obscures the light of the divine favor from himself, none the less my loving-kindness always keeps the trace of that blessedness in that man for eternal life: he multiplies this blessedness as often as he strives with devotion to attend the sacraments'.

9. After receiving communion, one day while she was meditating with what great care one should guard the mouth, as it in particular among the other parts of the body is the receptacle of the precious mysteries of Christ, she was instructed by this analogy: if someone does not guard the mouth from idle, untruthful, ugly, slanderous words and so on, she comes impenitent to holy communion and in such fashion receives Christ—as far as she can—like someone who buries a visitor on his arrival by piling up stones on the doorstep, or hits him on the head with a hard crow-bar! Anyone who reads this should consider with a deep sob of compassion what congruity there is of such great savagery with such great goodness, that he who came for human salvation with such great mildness, is so cruelly persecuted by those who were to be saved. It is possible to have similar thoughts about any other sin.

10. One day when she was about to receive communion, when she thought she was not prepared and the time was already at hand, she said to her soul, 'Here is the bridegroom already calling you, and how can you go to meet him, not prepared with any adornment of suitable merits?' Then pondering again much more on her own unworthiness, completely distrusting herself and putting her hope in God's loving-kindness, she said to herself, 'What's the use of putting it off? Even if I were left to my own efforts for a thousand years, I would not prepare myself suitably; since I can

have nothing of myself which can in any way lead to such a costly preparation. But I shall go to meet him with humility and trust; and when he sees me from afar, prompted by his own love, he has the power to send to meet me so that, worthily prepared, I shall be able to be brought into his presence'. Going forward with this intention, she kept the eyes of her heart fixed on her ugliness and unkempt state.

11. And when she had come a little closer, the Lord appeared, looking on her with a glance of mercy or rather of love, and sent to meet her, suitably to prepare her, his own Innocence with which he dressed her as a soft white shift. He sent his own Humility, by which he deigned to be associated with such unworthy beings, to dress her in it as a violet tunic. He sent his own Hope, by which he pants and burns for the embraces of the soul, to adorn her in green. He sent his own Love, by which he is swayed in his soul, to envelop her in a golden cloak; he sent his own Joy, with which he delighted in her soul, to crown her with a jeweled crown; finally, he sent his own Trust, by which he deigned to lean on a lowly creation of frail human nature when it was his delight to be with the children of men,[12] to provide her with shoes. And thus he brought her worthily into his presence.

12. After she had received communion, while she was withdrawn into the inmost depths of her being, the Lord appeared to her in the guise of a pelican, just as it is usually painted, piercing its heart with its beak. When she said in astonishment, 'My Lord, of what are you trying to convince me through this analogy?', the Lord replied, 'To consider by what incalculable goads of love am I compelled when I offer you such an outstandingly noble gift: for if it were not improper to say so, I would rather remain dead after [giving] this gift than withhold this gift from a loving soul. Also, consider in what an excellent way your soul, having received this gift, is restored to life which lasts eternally, just as the little pelican chick is restored to life from the blood of its father's heart'.

[12]Prv 8:31.

13. Again, one day when a sermon on the divine righteousness was being preached at great length, she took it so seriously that she trembled and greatly feared to approach the divine sacraments. By the goodness of God these words put heart into her: 'If you fail to look with inner eyes upon my goodness that has been shown you in innumerable ways, at least see with physical eyes in how small a pyx I am enclosed when I come to meet you. Know for certain that the rigor of my righteousness is thus completely enclosed in the gentleness of my mercy, which I worthily extend to the human race in the sustenance of this sacrament'.

14. Again, another time but at a similar moment and on a not dissimilar occasion, his divine loving-kindness enticed her to taste the sweetness of his delight with these words: 'Note the tiny shape of this substance in which I manifest to you all my divine and human natures, and compare its size with the size of the human body, and from that gauge the courtesy of my goodness. For just as the human body surpasses my body in size—that is, the size of the species of bread beneath which my body subsists—so my mercy and love draw me in this Sacrament to allow the loving soul, to a certain extent, to have the advantage over me, just as the human body has the advantage over my body in size'.

15. Another day, while the saving victim was being offered, the Lord again further intervened to commend his great courtesy, saying, 'Do you not observe that the priest who is offering the host has pushed up his arm band out of reverence in handling the sacrament, and is handling my body with his bare hands? Understand from this that although, as is right, I look with kindly regard on those efforts which are made to my glory, such as prayers, fasts, vigils and such like, none the less (even if it does not seem so to the less perceptive) I present myself to my chosen with a stronger emotion of compassion when, driven by the stings of human weakness, they flee to my mercy, just as there you see the priest's hand of flesh as more intimate than his arm band'.

16. Another time, when the bell was ringing at communion and the chant was being intoned, feeling herself less prepared than was

right she said to the Lord, 'Here you are, my Lord, already coming to me, and why have you not, as you could, sent me the jewels of devotion, so that I might come to meet you more fitly prepared for you?' The Lord replied, 'The bridegroom sometimes takes greater pleasure in seeing the white neck of his bride than when it is hidden with a necklace, and he takes even more pleasure in touching her well-turned hands[13] than in seeing them adorned with gloves. So I sometimes take more pleasure in the virtue of humility than in the grace of devotion'.

17. On one occasion, when many of the community, being prevented, refrained from communion, after she had received the mysteries she was for that reason rendering the Lord more devout thanks, saying, 'Invited to your banquet, I have come giving thanks'. The Lord spoke with most ravishing words, sweeter than honey and the honeycomb,[14] saying, 'Know that I longed for you with my whole heart'. Then she said, 'Lord, what glory does your divinity delight to gain from my chewing your spotless sacraments with my unworthy teeth?' The Lord replied, 'The love of one's own heart makes a friend's words delightful; thus I consider that, out of my own love, I delight to take pleasure in certain things for which my chosen have sometimes little taste'.

18. Another time, during the distribution of the sacrament, she strongly desired to see the host and was prevented from doing so by the crowds of those approaching the altar. She understood that the Lord was gently inviting her and saying, 'The sweet secret that concerns us must be unknown to those who are far from me. But you—if it pleases you to know—draw near and experience the taste of that hidden manna,[15] not by seeing but by eating'.

19. When she saw one of the Sisters approaching with great fear to take the life-giving sacrament, and turned away because of disgust, as if in anger, the Lord gently expostulated: 'Do you not consider

[13]Sg 5:14.
[14]Ps 18:11.
[15]Rv 2:17.

that I am owed no less justly the reverence of honor than the sweetness of love? But since the failing of human weakness cannot accomplish both equally in one emotion, since you are members one of another[16] it is right that what someone lacks in herself should be recovered by another. For instance, someone who with too much sweet love yields to less feeling of reverence should rejoice that this is made up for her by another who extends greater reverence, and should in return long for that other one to receive the comfort of divine unction'.

20. Another time, when she saw another nun trembling with fear for the same reason and was praying for her, the Lord replied, 'I could wish my chosen did not think me so cruel, but would believe that they would receive it as good, even as excellent, if they show me some service at great cost. For instance, someone offers a sacrifice to God at great cost when he has no taste for devotion but still serves God in prayers, genuflections and the like, and beyond this trusts in the benign loving-kindness of God, that he will however accept it with pleasure'.

21. Again, she was praying for someone who was complaining that the infusions of the grace of devotion took place less often on the day she was to receive communion than on certain other, even ordinary days. The Lord replied, 'This does not happen by chance but providentially. For when I infuse the grace of devotion on ordinary days and also at unexpected times, I strive through this to raise the human heart to me, which would [otherwise] perhaps remain in its sluggish state. But when I withdraw my grace on feast days or at the time of communion, the hearts of my chosen are greatly aroused by the will of their desires or by humility. Hence such eagerness—such contrition—profits more for their salvation than the occasional grace of devotion'.

22. When she was praying for someone who had omitted to receive the sacrament of the Lord's body for a trivial reason, that is, in case some people seeing her might be scandalized, she received an answer

[16]Rom 12:15.

in the form of this analogy: 'Just as a person who detects an obvious stain on the hand immediately washes the hands, but after washing not only are they washed clean of the obvious stain but also the hands as a whole are rendered cleaner; so it happens sometimes to my chosen. I allow them to fall into some trivial fault so that, penitent because of that, they become more pleasing to me from humility. But some frustrate my kindly purpose when they neglect their inner beauty, which I confirm after penitence, and are eager for the outer cleanliness which depends on human judgment. That is, when they do not care that they are losing my grace, which they could obtain from receiving the sacrament, just in case they should be thought somewhat disreputable before humans, because they seem to prepare themselves less carefully to receive the sacrament'.

23. Another day too when she was about to receive communion, she was being invited by the Lord in her inmost being, as if she were in the heavenly palace, about to take her seat by God the Father in the kingdom of his glory and eat at his table with him. She saw herself as totally unprepared for this and not at all composed and, anxious, was trying to retreat. The Son of God seemed to come to meet her, to prepare her and conduct her to his secret mysteries. First, as if washing her hands in the forgiveness of sins, he handed over to her the cleansing power of the Passion. Then he unclasped his own jewels—necklace, bracelets and rings—with which he appeared adorned, and hung them on her, reminding her that with them she would go forward properly and not like a foolish woman who, out of impropriety and awkwardness, does not know how to step forward and rather acquires contemptuous ridicule than respect for her modesty. By these words she understood that those with the Lord's jewels approach like fools who, while brooding on their own imperfection, pray the Son of God to make it good for them; but after receiving his blessing they still remain as timid as before, because they do not have complete trust in the Lord's most sufficient and complete power to make up their deficiencies.

24. Another day, when she was about to receive communion, while she was offering the Lord the sacrifice of the Lord's body for the relief of all in purgatory, she perceived thereafter that a great

alleviation for the souls of the faithful had resulted. Then in great astonishment she said to the Lord, 'My most kindly Lord—I call you this by reason of your grace—although (alas) I am quite unworthy, none the less you always deign to visit me with your presence, or rather to dwell within me. Whence comes it that you do not always bring about such an effect through me as I am now experiencing after the reception of your most holy body?' The Lord replied, 'Just as when a king lives in his palace, access is not readily granted to everyone[17] but when, vanquished by love for the queen who lives nearby, he deigns to descend from his palace into the city in order to visit her, all the citizens and inhabitants of that city, by reason of the queen, enjoy more easily and freely the generosity of his regal magnificence and rejoice in his riches; so when I am vanquished by the goodness and sweetness of my Heart, I bend down through the life-giving Sacrament of the Altar to any of the faithful who is without mortal sin, and to all who dwell in heaven, on earth and in purgatory is granted the increase of an inestimable blessing'.

25. Another day, as she was about to receive communion, she fell into the desire to plunge herself into the deepest valley of humility and lie there hidden, out of reverence for that astonishing courtesy by which the Lord shares his precious body and blood with his chosen. Then that deepest humiliation by which the Son of God descended to limbo to lay it waste became clear to her. Then entering into the union of that descent, it seemed to her that she had descended to the depths of purgatory. And there, sinking down as much as she could, she understood that the Lord was saying to her, 'In the reception of the sacrament I shall draw you towards me in such a way that you will draw with you all to whomsoever the fragrance of your desires[18] extends, that clings ineffable to your garments'.

26. After this promise, whenever at the reception of the sacrament she longed that the Lord would grant her as many souls from purgatory as the number of parts into which the host was broken in

[17] RB 58.4.
[18] Cf. Sg 1:3.

her mouth, and consequently tried to break it up into very many parts, the Lord said to her, 'That you may understand that the effects of my mercy are more than all my works[19] and that there is no one who can exhaust the abyss of my loving-kindness, look, I grant that by the ransom of this life-giving sacrament you shall receive much more than you venture to pray for'.[20]

27. Another day when about to communicate she withdrew herself from it even more than usual because of her unworthiness. She implored the Lord to receive that holy Host on her behalf in his own person and incorporate it with himself and then breathe into her out of the noble respiration of his most delightful breath, minute by minute, as much as he knew was appropriate to her littleness. Thence when she had rested for a while in the bosom of the Lord as it were beneath the shadow of his arms, in such a way that her left side seemed to lean against the blessed right side of the Lord,[21] a little later she raised herself up and perceived that from the loving wound in the Lord's most holy side she had contracted a pink scar on her left side. After this when she was approaching to receive the body of Christ, the Lord himself seemed to receive that sacred host in him with his divine mouth. Passing through her inmost being it emerged from the wound in Christ's most holy side and, like a dressing, fitted itself over that same life-giving wound. Then the Lord said to her, 'See how this host unites you to me in such a way that it covers up your scar from one side and my wound from the other, and becomes a dressing for both of us. You should change this dressing every day, as if cleaning it, by reciting devoutly the hymn "Jesus our redemption"'.[22] After this it was his pleasure that, in proportion, as it were, with the growth of her desire, she should increase her devotion day by day, so that on the first day she read this hymn once, on the second she read it twice and on the third day thrice, until the day when she again received communion.

[19] Ps 144:9.

[20] Collect for the Eleventh Sunday after Pentecost, *Omnipotens sempiterne Deus.*

[21] Bernard of Clarivaux, SC 51:5.

[22] Hymn for the Feast of the Ascension.

CHAPTER NINETEEN

A REVELATION ON THE PRAYER AND SALUTATION OF MARY THE MOTHER

1. Once at the time of prayer, when presenting herself before God she asked what he would most like her to meditate on at that time, the Lord replied, 'Stand beside my mother who sits at my side, and strive to praise her'. Then she devoutly greeted the Queen of heaven with this verse, 'Paradise of pleasure' and so on,[1] praising in her that she was the most delightful dwelling-place which the unsearchable Wisdom of God, to whom every creature is known, chose among the pleasures of his fatherly delights to dwell in. She prayed her to win for her a heart made charming by the variety of its virtues, so that God would take pleasure in dwelling in her too. At this the Blessed Virgin seemed to bend down as if to plant in her heart while she prayed the varied flowers of virtues: the rose of charity, the lily of chastity, the violet of humility, the heliotrope of obedience and the like. By this she intimated how ready she is to hear the prayers of those who call upon her.

2. And when, following that up, she again greeted her with the verse, 'Rejoice, model of virtue' and so on, praising in her that, more than all human beings, she had ruled her household of affections, moral dispositions, senses and all other impulses with such

[1]Cf. Gn 2:8.

great care that she rendered most fitting service to the Lord who was lodging in her, so much so that she never did anything unfitting in thought, word, or deed. She prayed that she too might win the same for herself. At this the Virgin Mother seemed to dispatch her affections in the guise of tender young girls, as if she were instructing them that they should all join themselves with all the affections of the woman who was praying and should exert themselves to serve the Lord with them and be eager to make up for them, in case those [her affections] were accomplishing less. Through this she gave her to understand how ready she is to help those who call upon her.

When this interlude had come to an end she said to the Lord, 'Since you, my brother, became human to make up for all human shortcomings, deign now on my behalf to make it up to your most blessed Mother if I have in any way performed her praises unworthily'. At these words the Son of God rose up with deepest reverence and coming before his Mother he knelt and greeted her most fittingly and most lovingly bowing his head, so that it was right for her to welcome [Gertrud's] service, whose imperfection was so fully made up by her most loving son.

3. The next day, when she was praying in similar terms, the Virgin Mother appeared to her in the presence of the ever-to-be-venerated Trinity, in the likeness of a white lily with, as is usual, three petals—one upright, two drooping. By this she was given to understand that the blessed Mother of God herself is thus worthily called 'the white lily of the Trinity', because above every creature she most fully and worthily received in herself the virtues of the honored Trinity, which not even the least speck of venial sin had ever stained. For by the upright petal was denoted the omnipotence of God the Father; by the two drooping petals, the wisdom and goodness of the Son and Holy Spirit, whom she is most like. Thence also she understood from the Blessed Virgin that if anyone greeting her devoutly called her 'white lily of the Trinity and brightest rose of heavenly loveliness', she would manifest in him most strikingly what powers she holds from the omnipotence of the Father; and what great knowledge she has for the salvation of humankind from the wisdom of the Son; and how immeasurably fertile she is in the bowels of loving-kindness from the goodness of the Holy Spirit.

The Blessed Virgin added, 'Also I shall appear to anyone who greets me in this way at the moment of death in the full bloom of such great beauty that for his wonderful consolation I shall provide him with heavenly loveliness'. From then onwards she decided to greet the blessed Virgin, or her image, with these words: 'Hail, white lily of the shining, ever-tranquil Trinity, and brightest rose of heavenly loveliness; from you the King of Heaven willed to be born, and of your milk he willed to be fed. Feed our souls with divine infusions'.

CHAPTER TWENTY

HER PRIVILEGED AFFECTION FOR THE LORD, AND HER SALUTATION OF THE IMAGE OF THE BLESSED VIRGIN MARY

1. It was her custom, as it is of lovers, to apply to her beloved all that pleased or delighted her. And so whatever she heard read or chanted in praise or salutation of the Blessed Virgin or of other saints, which could gently sway her love, through it she always concentrated more on the Kings of kings, the Lord who is, as was most right, above all, the one and only beloved and chosen one, than on the very saints whose feast or commemoration was being celebrated. And so on the feast of the Lord's Annunciation too, when the Blessed Virgin was repeatedly praised in the sermon and no mention was made of the most saving work of the Lord's Incarnation, she found this irksome and, returning from the sermon, while she was walking past the altar of the glorious Virgin, in greeting her sensed that she was not completely moved by gentle love towards that mother of all grace. Rather, in every salutation and praise of hers, she was always concentrating[1] more lovingly on Jesus, blessed fruit of her womb. Because of this she began to fear that she was incurring the wrath of so powerful a queen. The kindly comforter softly set her

[1] *intendere*; for the monastic concept of *intentio cordis* see Michael Casey, 'Intentio Cordis: RB 52.4', *Regulae Benedicti Studia* 6/7 (1981) 103–120.

fear aside, saying, 'Do not be afraid, dearest, that your greeting or praise of my dear Mother is such that you concentrate more on me: she greatly delights in this. But, since your conscience troubles you for this, another time be eager to greet before the altar the image of my chaste Mother with more devotion, leaving my own image ungreeted'.

She replied, 'Far be it from me, Lord, my only or rather complete Good! for my heart can never consent to this, that I should abandon you, on whom depends all the salvation or rather the very life of my soul, and that I should be able to direct my affection to greet someone else!' The Lord gently replied, 'Give me your consent now, my love. And as often as you greet my mother in this way and pass me over, I shall accept it and reward it as that perfection with which some truly faithful person readily leaves me, the hundredfold of all hundredfolds, for my greater glory'.

CHAPTER TWENTY-ONE

THE PEACEFUL REPOSE OF THE LORD

1. On the first Sunday after Trinity, the Lord appeared to her in a garden charming with flowery greenness, as if reclining at noon[1] and sitting on a royal throne he had been sweetly sleeping, drunk as it were from the wine[2] of charity. Flinging herself at his feet she kissed them affectionately again and again as was her custom. She caressed her beloved in various ways but for three days could win none of her customary enjoyment of him. And so on the fourth day during Mass she was unable any longer to bear her beloved's sleeping. She rose from his feet and in a paroxysm of ardor rushed at his breast, for which she burned with desire.[3] By the power of her love she strove to break in on her beloved's sleep. Aroused by this the Lord gently embraced her with both arms and, drawing her strongly to himself, said 'Look, now I am holding what I desired![4] For just as the fox wanting to catch birds flattens herself on the ground as if dead, and the little birds fly more freely above her and when they begin to peck her they are soon caught by her; so I too, burning with love for you, used this analogy by which I gain total possession of you when you launch yourself at me'.

[1]Sg 1:6.

[2]Ps 77:65.

[3]Gregory, Homily 25 *in Evangelia* (*Forty Gospel Homilies*, CS 123:188).

[4]Office of Saint Agnes.

CHAPTER TWENTY-TWO

THAT SICKNESS EXCUSES NEGLIGENCES

1. Another time, prevented because of sickness from keeping the full rigor of her Order, she had sat down to hear Vespers. From simultaneous longing and sorrow of heart she said to the Lord, 'Would it not, Lord, be more praiseworthy for you if right now I were among the convent in choir, with time for prayers and toiling at the other regular exercises, than as I am now, held back by this weakness and negligently wasting so much time?' The Lord replied, 'The bridegroom surely does not seem to you to take less pleasure in his bride when he enjoys her in privacy and delightful quiet and often drinks of her desired embraces,[1] than when he takes pride in her going forth in all her finery for public display?' From this she understood that at that time the soul goes into public in all her finery, as it were, when she is engaged in eagerness of good works to the glory of God. But at another time it rests as in private with its spouse when it is prevented by physical troubles from such pursuits. For then, deprived of the delights of its own senses, it is abandoned to the divine will alone. And thence the Lord takes so much the greater pleasure in a person, the less that person finds anything in himself in which he can vainly take pleasure or pride.

[1]Bernard of Clairvaux, SC 14:5.

CHAPTER TWENTY-THREE

A THREEFOLD BLESSING

1. One day when she was taking part in the Mass as devoutly as she could and it had reached the *Kyrie eleison*, it seemed to her that the angel, appointed her guardian by God, caught her up in his arms like a little child and presented her to God the Father to be blessed, saying, 'Bless your little daughter, Lord God the Father'. At this, when God the Father said nothing for a while as if he considered it beneath him to bless such a little thing, she examined herself and began with shame to turn over in her mind her worthlessness and unworthiness. Then the Son of God rose up and handed over as recompense the totality of his own most holy way of life. Then it seemed to her as if she were decked out in splendid, elaborate garments and thus had grown up to the measure of the fullness of Christ.[1] Then God the Father, too, bent down with most kindly readiness to be appeased and gave her a threefold blessing with threefold remission of all her sins of thought, word and deed which she had committed against his omnipotence. Then in thanksgiving she offered God the Father all the most holy way of life of his Only-begotten. Then every single jewel with which her clothes seemed to be adorned, combining together, seemed to make resound a most pleasing and delightful melody in everlasting praise of God

[1]Eph 4:13.

the Father. By this she was given to understand how most welcome it is to God the Father when someone offers him the most perfect way of life of his Son.

After this the angel mentioned above presented her in the same way to the Son of God, saying, 'Son of the King, bless your sister'. From him too she received a threefold blessing in remission of all that she had committed against the wisdom of God. Finally he presented her to the Holy Spirit, saying, 'Lover of humankind, bless your betrothed'. By him too she was given a threefold blessing in remission of all the sins by which she had offended against the goodness of God. Therefore anyone who wishes can concentrate on these nine blessings at the *Kyrie eleison*.

CHAPTER TWENTY-FOUR

THE RESULT OF CONCENTRATION ON SINGING THE PSALMS

1. One saint's day she was concentrating on devoutly chanting the canonical Hours in praise of God and of the saint in question. All the words she was chanting appeared like a sharp lance stretching from her own heart to the Heart of Jesus Christ. In penetrating to the very marrow, they moved her inestimably with most pleasurable delight. For from that lance, as if from its tip, rays seemed to be scattered like the most brightly glowing stars. As they reached each of the saints they made them resplendent with the wonderful beauty of fresh glory. But particularly that saint whose feast was being celebrated appeared, made bright by wonderful glory of unmatched splendor. From the lower end of the lance also appeared an increase of special grace for all who dwell on earth and help of refreshment for souls in purgatory, to be poured out flowing abundantly like a sudden shower of little drops.

CHAPTER TWENTY-FIVE

SERVICE OF THE DIVINE HEART

1. Another time she was earnestly trying to offer the individual notes and words with concentration, but was too often hindered in this by human frailty.[1] She grew sad and said to herself, 'What good can come from such earnest endeavor to someone who possesses so much inherent instability?' The Lord could not bear her sorrow and presented to her, as if with his own hands, his deified heart in the likeness of a burning lamp, saying, 'Here I hold out my heart, sweetest instrument of the ever-worshipful Trinity, before the eyes of your mind. You will entrust to it all that you cannot sufficiently complete by yourself, to be completed in trust on your behalf. And thus all will appear before my eyes perfect in every way. For, as in the parable, like the faithful servant[2] who stands always ready by his lord to carry out whatever he pleases, so my Heart will from now on be always with you for this purpose, to compensate on your behalf at any time for all your negligences'.

2. Astonished and terrified out of her wits at such an unheard-of act of the Lord's courtesy, she judged it quite inappropriate that the Lord's Heart, the most worthy treasure-chest of godhead that contains every good, should deign to stand by such a little thing,

[1] Collect for the Fourth Sunday after Epiphany.

[2] Lk 12:37.

like a servant by his lord, to make up for her own negligences. The Lord kindly met her faintheartedness and deigned to put heart into her by means of this analogy: 'It is as if you had a very resonant and agile voice and moreover took very great delight in singing. If you were standing next to a bad singer, who had a very hoarse and grating voice, so much so that she could hardly produce any sound even with great difficulty, you would certainly be angry that she did not entrust to you, who were supremely competent and very ready to chant, what she was having such trouble in producing. Similarly it is beyond doubt that my divine Heart recognizes human frailty and instability, and earnestly hopes, ever waiting with inestimable desire, that you, if not by words at least by a gesture, may entrust to it the task of compensating for you and completing what you cannot complete on your own. But just as it prevails very easily by almighty power, and knows most excellently by unsearchable wisdom, so also from the sweetness of its inherent goodness it desires to fulfill most excellently this task with most devoted joy'.

CHAPTER TWENTY-SIX

THE SOUL'S ABUNDANCE FROM GOD'S HEART

1. After this, one day while she was recollecting with gratitude the extremely munificent gift already mentioned, she yearningly asked the Lord how long he would deign to preserve it for her. The Lord replied, 'As long as you want to keep it you shall never mourn my taking it away from you'. Then she said, 'How can it be, O God, author of miracles beyond price, that I am aware of your deifying Heart in the likeness of a lamp hanging in the midst of my own heart, even though (alas!) most unworthy? And yet, whenever, thanks to the favor of your grace, I have deserved to approach you, I rejoice that I have found it within you, offering me abundance of every delight!'. The Lord replied, 'Just as when you want to grasp something you extend your hand, and then when you have grasped what you wanted you withdraw it, so I, sick with love[1] for you, extend my Heart to draw you back to me when you turn towards exterior things. But when by consenting to me in the depths of your being you remember to concentrate on me, I once more draw back my Heart to myself and from it I offer you the entertainment of all its varied virtues'.

[1]Sg 5:8.

2. Then meditating with great wonder and simultaneous gratitude on God's great freely-given goodness towards her, and thinking of the many-faceted worthlessness of her own failings, she submerged herself with the greatest self-abasement into the deepest vale of the humility that was known to her, and thought of herself as utterly unworthy of every grace. When she had lain low for a while in hiding, the Lord who, although he dwells on high,[2] none the less takes pleasure in generously imparting his grace to the humble, was seen to send down a sort of golden reed[3] from his Heart, which appeared in the likeness of a lamp hanging down above her soul thus pressed low in the valley of humility. Through this reed he poured into her in miraculous fashion the overflowing bounty of all that is desirable. For example, if she through recollecting her failings grew humble, the Lord immediately had mercy on her and poured into her from his own most blessed Heart the blossoming spring growth of his own divine virtues. Destroying all her failings, it never allowed them to show their faces before the eyes of his divine loving-kindness. In the same way, if she desired peace or adornment or anything else that one can think of as desirable and charming to the human heart, at once they all flowed into her, most delightfully and pleasurably, through that reed.

3. Having taken sweet pleasure for some time in such delights, and indeed while with the cooperation of God's grace she was being fitly arrayed and completely perfected in all the virtues (not hers however but the Lord's), she heard in her heart a most sweet voice, as of a harpist making delightful music on her harp,[4] saying, 'Come to me as mine. Enter me as mine. Remain with me as mine!' She understood the gist of this song by a honey-sweet insight from the Lord: 'Come to me as mine, for I, loving you, desire you as bride, dearest to my heart, to be with me always: therefore I call you. Again, since my delights are in you, I desire you to enter me, just as a young man desires the delight of his heart to be perfected in

[2]Ps 112:5.

[3]*fistulam*, the eucharistic reed used by the priest in the Middle Ages to drink the consecrated wine.

[4]Rv 14:2.

him. Again, since I, who am Love and God, have chosen you, I desire that you remain with me in an indissoluble union, just as a man is reluctant to lose his breath, which he cannot live without for a moment'. Among these most delightful pleasures she perceived that in an inestimably wonderful fashion she was being drawn to the Lord's Heart through the same reed that has been often mentioned. And in this way she found herself by happy chance in the innermost being of her bridegroom and the Lord her God. And there what she sensed, what she saw, what she heard, what she tasted and what she touched, was known to her alone and to him who deigned to admit her to such a superexcellently sublime union with himself, Jesus the bridegroom of the loving soul, who is God, blessed above all for ever.[5]

[5]Rom 9:15.

CHAPTER TWENTY-SEVEN

THE BURIAL OF THE LORD

1. On Good Friday when the burial of the Lord was being celebrated after the Office[1] she was praying the Lord that he would deign to be buried in her soul as a perpetual dwelling-place. Consenting most kindly, the Lord said, 'I myself, who am called "the rock",[2] shall be the stone at the entrances of all your senses and to guard them I shall set soldiers, that is, my affections, who will also guard your heart from all perverse affections and function in you according to my power for my eternal praise'.

2. After this, one day while she was observing a certain person's action that she had judged too harshly (so she feared), and being filled with compunction for this she was saying to the Lord, 'Lord, you have fortified the site of my heart with soldiers but, alas, I fear the site is deserted and they are absent, since I have judged this action of my neighbor's so harshly'; the Lord replied, 'How can you say that the site is deserted and they are absent, since in this very act you were aware of their power? For anyone who wants to cleave to me must rightly take no pleasure in what displeases me'.

[1] At Helfta in the thirteenth century this consisted of the 'burial' of a cross, rather than of a consecrated host, and of the chanting of two responses, *Ecce quomodo* and *Sepulto Domino* (now the sixth and ninth responses of Holy Saturday). See Solange Corbin, *Le déposition liturgique du Christ au Vendredi Saint* (Paris, 1960).

[2] 1 Cor 10:4.

CHAPTER TWENTY-EIGHT

THE CLOISTER OF THE LORD'S BODY

1. While at Vespers they were chanting 'I saw water proceeding forth', the Lord said to her, 'Look at my Heart; this will abide as your temple. Now search through the other parts of my body and choose for yourself other work areas[1] where you may live according to the Rule, for my body will from now on be your cloister'. She replied, 'Lord, I do not know how to search further or to choose, for I have found such delightful fecundity in your sweetest Heart which you deign to call my temple, that outside it I can receive no peace or refreshment, two things which do seem rather necessary in the cloister'. Then the Lord said, 'If you like, you may have those two qualities supremely in my Heart, for you have understood of others that they did not leave the temple, eating within it, and some such as Dominic also sleeping there. Choose, however, other things which seem useful for the cloister'. Then at the Lord's command she chose the Lord's feet for a periphery or ambulatory; for the workshop the Lord's hands; the Lord's mouth for parlor or chapter-house; the Lord's eyes for the classrooms where one reads; the Lord's ears for the place of confession. By this the Lord taught her that she ought always

[1] *officinas*.

climb up to it after every lapse, as if up the five steps of humility which are symbolized by these five epithets: 'I, worthless, a sinner, poor, wicked and unworthy, come to you, the overflowing abyss of loving-kindness, to be washed from every stain and purified from every sin. Amen'.

CHAPTER TWENTY-NINE

CLINGING TO THE LORD AND GREETING HIM

1. Once, turning over in her mind various examples of her instability, she turned to the Lord and said, 'It is good for me to cling[1] to you alone, my beloved'. Then the Lord bent down and embraced her, saying, 'It is always delightful for me too to cling to you, my beloved'. As he said this, all the saints rose up and offered their merits before the throne in reverence for the Lord, that he might grant them to her soul, so that she might become a fitter dwelling-place for him. From this she understood how easily the Lord bends down to the soul and how willingly the company of the saints waits upon him for that purpose, so that their own merits may compensate for the soul's unworthiness.

2. Hence when out of her desires' affection she said, 'I a worthless little human, greet you, most loving Lord', she received this reply from God's sweetest loving-kindness: 'I too greet you in return as my most loving [one]'. Through this she understood that as often as someone says to God with intent devotion 'my

[1]Ps 72:28.

beloved' or 'sweetest' or 'most loving' or the like, he often receives from him a response from which he will have a privilege of special glory in heaven, just as John the Evangelist has a special glory on earth in being called 'the disciple whom Jesus loved'.[2]

[2]Jn 21:7.

CHAPTER THIRTY

THE USE OF THE WILL; THE OFFERING OF THE HEART; AND VERY MANY ADDITIONAL POINTS WHICH SHE PERCEIVED IN HER UNDERSTANDING CONCERNING CERTAIN PHRASES OF THE DIVINE OFFICE; AND ALSO SOME OTHER INCIDENTAL POINTS

1. During the Mass 'Come and show [thy face]',[1] the Lord appeared as if all honeyed with the sweetness of divine grace, exhaling a life-giving, divine breath, and descending from the lofty throne of his imperial glory, as if to infuse more copiously into anyone desiring it the influx of his divine grace through the feast of his sweet-flowing Nativity. Then she prayed for those entrusted to her, namely that the Lord would vouchsafe each one more powerful grace, and she received this reply: 'I have given each a golden reed[2] of such power that with it anyone may draw to herself from the depths of my deified Heart anything she desires'. She understood that this reed was one's own will. Through it a human being can claim for herself every spiritual good, both heavenly and earthly. For instance, when

[1]Mass for Ember Saturday in Advent.

[2]Cf. III.26.2 above and note.

aroused by desire a person wishes to be able to render God as much praise, thanksgiving, service and faithfulness as any of the saints has shown Him, the vast goodness of God accepts this wish as if performed. But the reed, too, is ennobled with a golden color while the person thanks God that he has vouchsafed so noble a will, with which one can be infinitely more enriched than the whole world with all its strength can perform.

From this she understood that all the women of the community who were standing round the Lord were drawing in the divine grace, each according to her capacity, as it were through the reeds bestowed in them. Some appeared to draw directly from the depths of the Divine Heart. But to others what they received came through the hands of the Lord and so the greater the distance they drew from the Heart, the more difficult it was for them to obtain their desires. And the nearer to the Lord's Heart they tried to come, the more easily, sweetly and abundantly they drank. Whence, by those women who drank immediately and directly from the Lord's Heart, are symbolized those who completely conform and subdue themselves to the divine will, desiring above all that the most praiseworthy will of God concerning themselves may be completely performed, in both spiritual and physical things. And these move the divine Heart towards themselves with such great efficacy that at a time foreordained by the Lord they receive a flood of divine delight as fully and delightfully as they have unreservedly entrusted themselves to his will. But by those who were trying to draw something through the Lord's other limbs, are signified those who according to their own desire attempt to win certain gifts of graces or fruits of virtues, according to the disposition of their own good pleasure. The more they rely on their own will, and the less they entrust themselves to divine Providence, the harder they have to work for their own desires.

2. And she offered the Lord her own heart in these terms: 'Here is my heart, Lord, withdrawn from every created thing; I offer it to you with my entire will, praying you to wash it in the virtuous water of your most sacred side, and to array it most fittingly in the precious blood of your sweetest Heart and to make it most becomingly fit for you in the warm spicy breath of your divine love'. The Son of God

appeared, offering God the Father her heart united with his own divine Heart in the likeness of a chalice, its two parts joined together with wax. When she saw this she said to the Lord with suppliant devotion, 'Most loving God, grant that my heart may be always at hand, like the flasks which are brought for lords' refreshment, so that you may always, as you please, have it clean for pouring in and pouring out whenever you wish, for whomever you please'.

The Son of God kindly accepted this and said to the Father, 'Holy Father, may this heart pour out, to your eternal praise, all that my Heart contained for dispensation in my human nature'. From then on, when she quite often offered her heart to the Lord through the words written above, it seemed to her that it was replenished sometimes in such a way that its outpouring through praises and thanksgivings was fit for the increase of joy for the dwellers of heaven, sometimes in such a way that it was also suitable for those on earth, for their progress, as is clear from what follows. For she understood from this time on that it was the Lord's pleasure that she should have such things written down for the profit of many.

3. In Advent she understood from the response 'Behold, the Lord our protector will come, the Holy One of Israel', that if anyone were disposed with her entire will to desire in her heart that every section of her life, both in prosperity and in adversity, should be ruled according to the most praiseworthy will of God, with such a thought by the mediation of God's grace she confers as great an honor on the Lord as he who places the royal crown on his head confers on the emperor.

4. Again, from the verse which is read in Isaiah, 'Arise, arise, stand up, Jerusalem',[3] she understood the profit which accrues to the Church Militant from the devotion of the chosen. For specifically when a single loving soul turns with its whole heart to the Lord with its entire will with which, if it had the power, it would most gladly make reparation to God for every injury that is a detriment to his honor and thus, burning with the torches of love in prayer, it clings caressingly to God, it pleases him so much that at length he

[3]Is 51:17.

is conciliated and spares the whole world. This is what is meant by the words 'You have drunk even to the bottom of the chalice'.[4] For by such means the severity of justice is completely transformed into the serenity of mercy. But by the words that follow, 'You have drunk even to the dregs',[5] it is implied that there can be no redemption[6] for the damned, who deserve the dregs of justice.

5. Again, from that verse in Isaiah 'You shall be glorified, while you do not go your own ways',[7] she understood that anyone who orders his words and deeds by deliberate thought and none the less considers there is no utility in them and refrains from what he would perhaps have liked, obtains from this a threefold blessing. First, that it is given to him to take a more pleasing delight in God, as it says: 'You shall take your delight in the Lord'.[8] Secondly, that harmful thoughts will have less power against him, as it says: 'I shall bear you up above the heights of the earth'.[9] Thirdly, that in the life eternal the Son of God imparts more fully to him than to others the fruit of his most holy way of life, in which he resisted every temptation with noble victory and conquered gloriously, as it says: 'And I shall feed you with the inheritance of Jacob your father'.[10]

Again, in the words of Isaiah, 'Behold his reward is with him',[11] she understood how the Lord himself in his love is the reward of the chosen, presenting himself so sweetly that the mind of the lover can assert with utmost truth that he is rewarded most worthily, far beyond every desert. 'And his work is before him'[12] when he entrusts himself totally to divine Providence and desires the will of God in every act; already, by the grace of God, he appears perfect in the eyes of God.

[4] Is 51:17.

[5] Ibid.

[6] Response of the Office of the Dead.

[7] Is 58:13.

[8] Is 58:14.

[9] Ibid.

[10] Ibid.

[11] Is 40:10.

[12] Ibid.

6. Again, from the verse 'Be sanctified, sons of Israel',[13] she understood that if anyone, in true penitence for all her sins of omission and commission with her whole heart bows in obedience to God's commandments, she is truly sanctified in the eyes of God and is found prepared, just as that leper was purified to whom the Lord said, 'I wish it: be purified'.[14]

7. Again, from the verse 'Sing unto the Lord a new song',[15] she understood that everyone who sings with devout concentration sings a new song to the Lord. For being already renewed because he receives grace from God by which he is able to concentrate on Him, he will be acceptable to God.

8. Again, from the verse 'The spirit of the Lord is upon me'[16] and later 'That I may heal the contrite of heart', she understood that since the Son of God had been sent by the Father to heal the contrite of heart, he was accustomed to make contrite his chosen with some burden, sometimes small, even concerning external matters, so that he might have the opportunity of healing them. But when he has turned to the soul for this reason, he does not heal that burden by which the heart is perhaps made contrite, for it is not harmful; but rather he heals whatever he finds in the soul that is damaging.

9. Again, from that verse 'In the splendors of the saints'[17] she understood that the light of the godhead is so great and so incomprehensible that if each of the saints, from Adam up to the most recent, singly perceived a single insight so bright, profound and extensive that no creature could ever possibly grasp it, so that no other could share in their own insight; even if the company of saints were a thousand times larger, none the less the godhead would remain unspent forever, beyond all reach of understanding.

[13]Response for the Vigil of Christmas.

[14]Mt 8:3.

[15]Is 42:10.

[16]Is 61:1.

[17]Ps 109:4.

And this is why it does not say 'in the splendor' but 'in the splendors of the saints; from the womb before the morning star I have begotten you'.[18]

10. Again, while they were chanting of a martyr, 'He who wishes to come after me',[19] she saw the Lord walking along a path charming with greenness and the beauty of flowers, but narrow and harsh with the thickness of thorns. She saw the likeness of the cross go before him, conveniently making the path wider by a separation of the thorns from each other, and she saw him turn back with a serene countenance, inviting those behind him and saying: 'He who wishes to come after me, let him deny himself, take up his cross, and follow me'. In the midst of this she understood that to each one their own trial is their own cross. For instance: for some the cross was that they were compelled by the goads of obedience to something which goes against their wishes; but for others, that they were hampered from what they wanted by the burdens of weakness; and thus other people have other trials. Thus everyone must take up their own cross to show their will to suffer gladly what goes against their wishes and none the less as far as possible they do not neglect to fulfill anything they know brings praise to God.

11. While they were chanting in the psalm the verse, 'The words of the wicked'[20] and so on, she understood that when someone guilty from human frailty is corrected for her guilt, if too much is said the words call forth God's mercy and become increase of the guilty one's merit.

12. When they were chanting 'Hail, Queen [of heaven]', through the phrase 'thy merciful eyes' she was hoping that she might be granted physical health. The Lord, as if smiling softly to himself, said, 'Do you not know that I look upon you with my most merciful gaze because you are physically chastised and mentally distressed?'

[18] Ps 109:3.

[19] Antiphon of the Third Nocturn of the Common of a Martyr, or Communion of the Mass *In virtute tua*; cf. Mt 16:24.

[20] Ps 64:4.

13. Again, on the feast of certain martyrs, while they were chanting 'the glorious blood',[21] she understood that, just as blood which is intrinsically abominable but because it is shed for Christ is praised in Scripture, in the same way that neglect of religious observances which results from obedience or brotherly love is so pleasing to God that it can be rightly called 'glorious'.

14. One time she understood that God in his hidden judgment sometimes allows that, when each corrupted person seeks by cunning temptation the knowledge of some secret from the chosen, he should sometimes receive an answer by which he becomes even more obstinate in the corruption of his error. This is to his disadvantage but acts as a test of the chosen. And so it says in Ezechiel, 'He who has set impurities in his heart, and the stumbling-block of iniquity before his face, and has come to the prophet, questioning him for me, I the Lord shall answer him in the multitude of his impurities, that he may be caught in his own heart'.[22]

15. Also from the words that are chanted of John, 'He has drunk deadly poison',[23] she understood that just as the virtue of faith preserved John unharmed by poison, so the consent of the will conserves the soul unspotted, however poisonous may be what makes its way into the heart against one's will.

16. From the versicle 'Grant, O Lord, this day',[24] she understood that in whatever a person entrusts himself to God, praying that He guard him from sin, even if in the hidden judgment of God it should seem to that person that he has transgressed gravely in something, none the less he never does transgress to such an extent that the grace of God does not sustain him like a staff, that he will always return the more easily to repentance.

[21] Response *Viri sancti* from the Common of Many Martyrs.

[22] Ez 14:4–5.

[23] Former Response for the feast of Saint John the Evangelist.

[24] Versicle for Prime.

17. While they were chanting the response 'In blessing',[25] as if in the person of Noah she stood by the Lord, demanding a blessing. When this had been obtained the Lord in his turn seemed to ask a blessing from her. From this she understood that a person blesses the Lord when in his thought he says that he is sorry that he ever offended his Creator, and demands his help to avoid it in future. At this blessing the Lord of heaven bowed deeply with joy and showed her that she was as acceptable to him, as if his entire well-being were perfected through her.

18. Again, from the verse 'Where is your brother Abel?'[26] she understood that the Lord requires from every religious anything done by a neighbor against religion, whose prevention he could somehow have effected, either by advising the person or counseling his superiors. That excuse some people make—'It is not my job to correct others' and 'I myself am worse than him'—does as little good before God as it did Cain, who said, 'Am I my brother's keeper?'[27] For everyone is bound in the eyes of God to restrain his brother from evil and urge him on to good. And as often as he neglects this against conscience, he transgresses against God. Nor does it do any good that he claims it has not been entrusted to him, for this has indeed been entrusted to him; beyond that, his own conscience shows him. And if he is negligent, God will require this from his soul, sometimes even more than from the soul of the superior who was not there or perhaps, if he was, did not notice. Thence Scripture threatens, 'Woe to the one who acts; woe, woe to the one who consents'.[28] He who keeps it secret incurs guilt by consenting since by exposure he could promote the praise of God.

19. From the response 'The Lord has clothed me',[29] she understood that he who in word or deed promotes religion and rationally

[25]Response for Sexagesima.

[26]Gn 4:9; Response for Septuagesima.

[27]Gn 4:9.

[28]Rom 1:32.

[29]From the Common of Virgins; cf. Is 61:10.

defends justice, clothes as it were the Lord in a garment at once serviceable and richly ornamented. And the Lord will reward him in the life eternal according to the generosity of his royal munificence by wrapping him in garments of joyfulness and for increase of his reward will adorn him with a crown of spiritual glory.[30] But in particular she understood that he who, promoting the best interests of religion, suffers setbacks, is so much the more acceptable to God, just as a garment that warms and also covers his nakedness is the more welcome to a poor man. Even if he who promotes religion has made no progress, others putting obstacles in his way, none the less his reward is not in the eyes of God lessened in the least.

20. While the response 'An angel of the Lord called'[31] was being chanted, she understood how the hosts of angels, whose help can be more than sufficient, surround the chosen to protect them. But the Lord in his fatherly foresight sometimes suspends that protection to allow the chosen to be tempted in something. By this means they would be rewarded the more gloriously, the more they triumph through their own strength, the angelic guard and protection being withdrawn.

21. Again, when they subsequently chant, 'The angel of the Lord called Abraham',[32] she understood that just as holy Abraham, having extended his arm to carry out obedience, deserved to be called by an angel, so when a chosen person applies his mind because of God to some task difficult for him and brings to bear his whole will, in an instant the delight of divine grace smiles on him and he deserves to be consoled by the testimony of his own conscience. And this is a bonus by which the totally unbounded generosity of God forestalls the eternal reward by which each one will receive his own reward according to his own labor.[33]

[30] Cf. Is 61:10.

[31] Response of Quinquagesima; cf. Gn 22:11.

[32] Ibid.

[33] 1 Cor 3:8.

22. Once when she was turning over in her mind the trials of her past life, she asked the Lord why he allowed her to be troubled at that time by certain people. She received this reply from him: 'When the father's hand wants to correct his son, the rod cannot resist him. So I would like my chosen never to blame the people by whom they are purified, but always regard my fatherly love. For I would not allow the lightest breeze to blow against them if I were not looking to their eternal salvation, which they shall receive in reward. But let them feel compassion for those who for the sake of their own purification are sometimes defiled'.

23. Another time, because of the difficulty of a certain task, she was saying to God the Father, 'Lord, I offer you this task through your only Son, in the power of the Holy Spirit, to your eternal praise'. Through her understanding she sensed in her the power of these words, specifically that for this intention she was miraculously ennobled above human reckoning and whatever was offered became acceptable to God the Father. To provide a comparison, just as anything seen through green glass appears green and again anything seen through red glass appears red, and so on, so anything offered through the Only-begotten is most pleasing and acceptable to God the Father.

24. When she was asking the Lord in her prayer what good it did her friends to pray for them so often, when she saw in them no benefit of her prayer, she was instructed by the Lord by this analogy: 'When a little child is brought back from the emperor endowed with vast estates, which of the onlookers immediately sees any fruit of that endowment in the boy's appearance? None the less it is no secret to the witnesses what sort of person, and how great, he will be from the riches granted him. Therefore do not be surprised that you cannot physically discern the fruit of your prayers, which I lay out to their greater benefit according to my eternal wisdom. The more often a prayer is made for someone the more greatly he is blessed, for no faithful prayer will remain fruitless, although its manner of fruition remains hidden from humans'.

25. As she wished to know what would be the fruit of directing one's thoughts to God, she was taught as follows: when someone directs his thoughts to God in meditation or reflection, before the throne of glory he presents to God a mirror, as it were, of wonderful brightness, in which the Lord gazes most gladly at his own image. For he is the dispatcher and director of all good things. When a person sometimes toils with some difficulty in such tasks because of obstacles, the harder he toils the more delightfully that mirror appears adorned in the sight of the ever-to-be-worshipped Trinity and of all the saints. And this shall remain forever to the glory of God and the perpetual exultation of his soul.

26. One feast day when she was prevented from chanting by a headache, she asked the Lord why he quite often allowed this to happen to her on feasts. She received this reply: 'Lest perhaps raised up by the pleasure of harmony you should be found less fit for my grace'. She replied, 'Your grace, Lord, could prevent that lapse in me'. The Lord said, 'It is more profitable for a person that the opportunity of a lapse be removed through the crushing of troubles, for from that her merit is doubled, that is, of patience and humility'.

27. Drawn one day by excessive love, she was saying to the Lord, 'Would that I had such a fire, Lord, that my soul could be melted like a completely liquefied substance, so that I could pour it all the more precisely into you!' The Lord replied, 'Your will is such a fire for you'. From these words she understood that through her will a person possesses the full effect of all desires that look towards God.

28. Since she often strove to obtain from the Lord by her prayers the eradication of vices, both in herself and in others, it often seemed to her that she could not entreat it more completely than to ask that the loving-kindness of God would mitigate that compulsion that results from evil habit—that is, that he would make it as easy for her to resist vice as if no difficulty had accrued from habit, which is called 'second nature'. For in this too she recognized the admirable plan of the divine loving-kindness concerning the salvation of the human race: for in order that an accumulation of eternal glory may accrue to someone more fully, He allows him to be quite heavily

attacked by very many vices so that he may the more happily be able to exult about his triumph.

29. During a sermon she had heard this statement enunciated: no human being is saved without the love of God, in that he must at least love Him enough to repent and refrain from sin. She reflected in her heart that many depart this world who seem to repent more out of fear of hell than love of God. The Lord said in reply, 'When I see in agony those who have ever been sweetly mindful of me, or who have done some good work in the very throes of death, I manifest myself to them as worthy of love with such kindliness that they repent from the innermost depths of their heart ever having offended me, and thence they are saved at that moment through such repentance. Therefore I would wish to be glorified by my elect for that courtesy, specifically that among my generic acts of kindness they should thank me also for that particular one'.

30. Sometimes while meditating she began to recognize her inner ugliness and to become so dissatisfied with herself that, anxious and troubled, she carefully considered how she could ever please God,[34] who saw so many stains in her. For where she detected one, the piercing eye of divinity perceived an infinite number. She was divinely consoled on this topic by this reply: 'Love makes pleasing'. She understood from this that if love has such power among earthly beings that sometimes the ugly, because of love, are pleasing to those by whom they are loved, and are also from time to time so pleasing that lovers, through the force of love, long to be like their beloveds, how then should we despair of him who is the God that is Love, that he is unable by the force of love to render pleasing those whom he loves?

31. Again, when she greatly desired, in accordance with the words of Saint Paul, to be dissolved and be with Christ,[35] and on this was uttering many groans to God from the depths of her heart, on one occasion she was comforted by this reply: as often as she conveyed

[34] 1 Cor 7:32.
[35] Phil 1:23.

with her whole heart her desire to be delivered from the prison of this death,[36] and in addition kept steadfast her will to abide in the body,[37] thc Son of God would add all his own most holy way of life to her own way of life and thence she would miraculously appear perfect in the eyes of God the Father.

32. One day when she was thinking over the many varied graces infused in her from God's generous loving-kindness, she thought that she was wretched and unworthy of every good thing. For she had received so many countless gifts from God but had spoilt them so negligently that it seemed she had harvested no fruit whatsoever[38] from them, neither in herself through their fruitfulness or through thanksgiving, nor in others among whom, if they had known of it, there would have been cause of edification or improvement of divine knowledge.

She was comforted on this point by this insight: sometimes the Lord does not pour forth the gifts of his graces into his chosen in such a way that he demands they harvest worthy fruit from every single one, since human frailty often prevents it. But since the overflowing loving-kindness and generosity of God cannot contain itself, even though he knows that a person is unable to make use of every single one, none the less he assiduously heaps up the accumulation of graces so that he may grant to that person the accumulation of blessedness in the future. Similarly as often happens with earthly possessions—which are sometimes granted to a little child who does not know how to expect to use them, so that later on as an adult he may have an abundance of goods—so the Lord, when he bestows a grace on his chosen in this life, is preparing for and granting to them some of that eternal fruition with which they will be blessed in heaven.

33. On one occasion while she was lamenting in her heart that she could not have as great a desire as was expedient for God's praise, she was divinely taught that it is quite sufficient for God, when he can

[36] Rom 7:24.

[37] Phil 1:24.

[38] Lk 8:14.

have no more, that a person should freely and willingly have a great desire; and in the eyes of God he has as great a desire as he would wish to have. And because that heart contains such a desire—that is, the will to have a desire—here especially does God delight more to dwell than ever a human being can dwell among the flowers of springtime loveliness.

34. On one occasion, prevented by physical weakness she had been for some days somewhat sluggish in concentrating on God. Recovering at last with heavily laden conscience, she was eager to confess this failing of hers to the Lord with humble devotion. And although she was afraid that she would have to struggle through a lengthy period of delay before she would recover the delight of divine grace, in an instant she suddenly sensed that the goodness of God was bending towards her in a most alluring embrace and saying, 'Daughter, you are always with me and all that is mine is yours'.[39] In these words she understood that, although a person sometimes fails out of human frailty to direct her attention to God, none the less the loving mercy of God does not fail to count all our works as worthy of eternal reward, if only the will is not turned away from God, and a person is often sorry for all those things which gnaw the conscience.

35. At one feast she was conscious of weakness and desired the Lord to temper it until after the feast, or at least in such a way that she should not be prevented from celebrating that feast. None the less, she entrusted herself completely to the divine will. On this she received the following reply from the Lord: 'In that you seek this gift from me and in addition entrust yourself to my will, you lead me to a garden of delights, set with flower beds and very lovely to me. But know that if I hear you in this, that you should not to be hindered from my service, then I follow you to the flower bed in which you take greater pleasure. But if I do not hear you, and you persevere in patience, then you follow me to the flower bed in which I take greater pleasure. For I find more loveliness in you

[39]Lk 15:31.

if you have desire with suffering than if you have devotion with pleasure'.

36. Once when she was pondering by what rationale some abound in such richness of spirit in the service of God while others remain so dry, she received this insight from God: 'That the heart was created by God to hold pleasures just as a pot that holds water; but if the pot holding water pours it out through tiny holes, eventually it can become so empty that the pot too remains dry. So if the human heart holding pleasure pours it out through the physical senses, that is, by seeing and hearing and also doing what it wants through the other physical senses, it can pour out so much that the heart will remain empty of pleasure in God. Anyone could experience this in themselves. When one wants to see something, or speak a single word in which there is little or no profit, if he does it at once he thinks nothing of it, for it slips out like water. But if he determines to hold it back because of God, it grows in his heart so much that he can hardly control it. Thence when a person has learnt to control himself in such matters, he becomes used to taking pleasure in God, and the harder the effort to do this, the more fruitfully he begins to take pleasure in God'.

37. Being unbearably oppressed within herself about some trivial matter, she offered up her desolation to God to his eternal praise at the elevation of the Host. Thence the Lord seemed to draw her soul to him through that sacred Host, as if through a lattice,[40] and she seemed to be reclining sweetly on the Lord's breast and he courteously spoke these words: 'In this reclining you shall breathe free from every annoyance. But whenever you go away, bitterness of heart will seize you again as a healthy antidote'.

38. Once when exhausted, her powers failing, she said to the Lord, 'What must be done about me, my Lord, or what do you intend to do with me?' The Lord replied, 'Just as a mother comforts her sons,[41] so shall I comfort you. And the Lord added, 'Have you not

[40] Cf. Sg 2:9.
[41] Is 66:13.

seen a mother caressing her son?' When she said nothing, failing to remember, the Lord reminded her that about six months before she had seen a mother caressing her little boy. He particularly impressed upon her three things which she had not noticed at the time she saw them. First, the mother often asked the little boy for a kiss, at which the little boy tried to stand up in spite of the feebleness of his limbs; He added that she should raise herself, with great effort, through contemplation to the enjoyment of his most delightful love. Second, the mother tested the little boy's will, saying 'Is this what you want? and is that what you want?', but doing neither! So God tests a person, sometimes allowing him to anticipate troubles that never actually happen. That the person consents from his will, however, is quite sufficient for God and makes him worthy of eternal reward. Third, of all those present no one understood the babbling of the boy, who could not yet form words, except for the mother. So God alone understands a person's intention and judges according to that—far differently than human beings who only pay attention to outer things.

39. Once, when the memory of past sins had so cast her down that she was doing all she could to be inconspicuous, the Lord bent down to her with such courtesy that all the court of heaven, as if astonished, was striving to call him back. To this the Lord replied, 'I cannot possibly restrain myself from pursuing her, for she attracts my divine Heart to her with such powerful cords of humility'.

40. Asking the Lord what he would like her to concentrate on at that moment, the Lord replied, 'I want you to learn patience'. For she was strongly disturbed for a particular reason. At this she said, 'How or by what means could I learn it?' Then the Lord, taking her up to himself like a kindly teacher holding a little pupil in his lap, put before her, as if in the form of three letters,[42] three things that ought to stimulate her to patience. At the first he said, 'Ponder with what great friendliness a person is summoned by a king who resembles him more than all others in every way. Thence think how much fondness towards you increases because

[42] That is, the ABC.

you suffer contumely like mine on my account'.[43] At the second he said, 'Again, ponder what respect the king's greatest friend, who is most like him in every way, obtains from the household. And from this think what glory is prepared for you in heaven for your patience'. At the third he said, 'Consider what solace comes to a friend from his most faithful friend's caressing sympathy, and from this think with what most pleasant caress I shall soothe you in heaven in return for the least thoughts that trouble you here'.

[43]Acts 5:41.

CHAPTER THIRTY-ONE

A PROCESSION WITH THE IMAGE OF THE CROSS

1. A procession which had been decreed because of the exigency of the weather[1] had taken place and as the convent was returning to choir the cross was carried before them. She understood that the Son of God was speaking from the cross and saying, 'Here am I with my army, come to beseech you, God the Father, in the form in which I reconciled all human nature'. With these words she was aware of the heavenly Father, calm with such a kindly readiness to be pleased, as if every human fault had been very worthily expunged one hundred times over. Then God the Father was also seen to raise the cross into the clouds with these words: 'This shall be the sign of the covenant between me and the earth'.[2]

2. Again, another time when wild winds were greatly afflicting the people and she with the others was invoking God's mercy again and again for this, but was aware of no result, she finally said to the Lord, 'Most kindly lover, how can you put off for so long the longings of many when I, although unworthy, have such confidence in your loving-kindness that [I believe] I alone could sway your mercy to

[1]Possibly the procession referred to in I.13.1.

[2]Gn 9:13.

greater things?' The Lord replied, 'It would not be astonishing that a father allowed his son to ask him for a penny, if each time he had a hundred marks set aside for his son. Thus do not be astonished that I put off hearing you all in this matter, for each time you pray for it, even with the least words or thoughts, I put aside for you far more than a hundred marks from the treasures of heaven!'

CHAPTER THIRTY-TWO

FREQUENT DESIRE; DISRUPTION OF SLEEP BY THE TEMPTING OF THE ENEMY

1. During Mass for the Dead, while the tract 'Like the hart' was being chanted and at the words 'My soul has thirsted' and so on she was meditating on her lukewarmness, she said to the Lord, 'Alas, Lord, that my desires for you, my true good, are so lukewarm that it is so rarely appropriate for me to say to you, "My soul has thirsted for you"'. The Lord replied, 'Not rarely but quite often do you say to me that your soul thirsts for me, for the loving-kindness of love, by which I love human salvation, drives me always to count my chosen as having desired me, whatever good things they desire, since every good lies hidden in me and flows out from me. For instance, if a person desires health, security, ease, wisdom and so on, I often count him as having desired me so that I may greatly pile up the merit of his reward. I make an exception if he has deliberately turned away from me, if for instance he desired to have wisdom so that he could take pride in it, or health so that he could carry out evil'. And the Lord added, 'Therefore it is very often my custom to weigh down my closest friends with weakness of body and desolation of mind and the like so that when they desire to gain the contrary good things, the burning love of my Heart is able to reward them more generously according to the good pleasure of my open-handedness'.

2. Similarly, another time she was divinely inspired and understood that sometimes the Lord, 'whose delights are to be with the sons of men',[1] finds nothing in a person in which He can take pleasure and appropriately deign to be present with him. Then He sends troubles or trials (both physical and spiritual) so that as a result He may have the opportunity of staying with him. For the Scripture of truth says, 'The Lord is near those whose heart is troubled'.[2] Again, 'I am with him in tribulation'.[3] In consideration on this and many similar things, a loving gratitude of human littleness is forced to cry out with all the affections of the heart those words of the apostle: 'Oh the height of the riches of the wisdom and knowledge of God, how incomprehensible are his judgments and unsearchable his ways'[4] which he has devised for the salvation of the human race!

3. One night she was asleep and was being delightfully visited by the Lord through a dream, so much so that from her fellowship with the presence of the Lord it seemed to her that she was crammed with more exquisite banquets. Waking from this she thanked the Lord, saying, 'Why, Lord, have I who am utterly unworthy deserved this more than others who are quite often so troubled through dreams that they even strike terror into others through their screams from time to time?' The Lord replied, 'My fatherly foresight plans to sanctify these people through suffering. If while awake they are eager to obtain ease for their bodies, and consequently deprive themselves of opportunities for reward, I out of my divine loving-kindness inflict trouble on them through their dreams so that at least in this way they may merit something.'

She replied, 'Surely, Lord, it would not be possible for them to win this merit because they suffer unintentionally and, as it were, against their will?' The Lord then replied, 'My kindness accomplishes this; for as it is seen in the world, people who deck themselves with glass and copper are perceived as adorned, but those

[1]Prv 8:31.

[2]Ps 33:19.

[3]Ps 90:15.

[4]Rom 11:33.

who are crowned with gold and precious stones are considered much richer. So it is with them'.

4. Once when she was reading the canonical Hours with less concentration, she realized that the ancient enemy of the human race was there. As if in mockery he was completing the rest of the psalm, 'Your testimonies are wonderful',[5] skipping the syllables as if in a hurry. When he had finished the verse, he added, 'Your Creator, Savior and Lover has made a good investment in that he gave you such quick speech that you are able to form so nicely any word you like for whatever you like, since in speaking to him you utter so hastily that in that psalm just now you left out numerous sounds, syllables and words!' She understood from this that the cunning enemy had so carefully counted up the individual sounds and syllables in that psalm, that he could bring a serious charge after death against those who are in the habit of saying the Hours hastily and without concentration.

5. Again, when hastily spinning, she let some little balls of wool fall and in the meantime was entrusting her work to God with pious intention, she saw a demon collecting those balls in evidence, as it were, of her guilt. At this when she called upon the Lord, he himself drove out the demon and rebuked[6] him for having had the audacity to intrude on a task that had from the first been entrusted to God.

[5] Ps 118:129.

[6] Lk 9:43.

CHAPTER THIRTY-THREE

THE FAITHFUL SERVICE OF THE LORD

1. Once, when she was burning for the Lord with greater desire, she said to the Lord, 'Ah, my Lord, could I pray to you now?' The most kindly Lord gently replied to her, 'Indeed, Lady and Queen, best of all you could command me; for I shall obey your will and desire in all things more readily than ever any servant can serve his mistress'. She said, 'The word of your most loving condescension is in all things inviolate, most kindly God. And yet since you condescend to show yourself so attentive to me, most unworthy, please tell me why my prayer is so often ineffectual?' The Lord replied, 'Suppose a queen says to her servant, "Give me the thread that is hanging down back there, above my left shoulder", thinking it is indeed there, although she cannot see behind her. The servant seeks to do what he has been ordered and when he sees the thread is not hanging above her left shoulder but above her right he at once picks it up where he finds it and gives it to his lady, thinking it more sensible than if he pulled a thread out of her tunic on the left side, to carry out her order! Similarly if at times I who am unsearchable wisdom do not hear your prayers[1] in the way you wish, there is no doubt that I always substitute more profitable things, although you, hindered by human frailty, cannot discern that they are better'.

[1]Cf. RB 20.7.

CHAPTER THIRTY-FOUR

THE PROFIT OF THE LORD'S OFFERING AND THAT OF THE SAINTS FOR HUMANKIND

1. Once, about to receive the body of Christ, while she was sorrowing that she was so unprepared, she prayed the Blessed Virgin and all the saints to offer on her behalf all the merit by which each one of them had been prepared for the reception of some grace. In addition she prayed the Lord Jesus Christ that he would condescend to offer on her behalf that perfection prepared with which, at the moment of the Ascension, he stood before God the Father to receive glorification. A little later while she was trying to find out what she had gained from this prayer, the Lord replied, 'This you have gained, that you now truly appear to all the citizens of heaven in that splendid apparel which you asked for yourself'. The Lord added, 'Why would you want to distrust that I, the all-powerful and most kindly God, would not be able to do what anyone even on earth could do? For if he has garments and splendid apparel he could dress his friend in them or something similar and thence could make that friend appear splendid in that same splendid apparel in which he shone himself'.

2. Then she remembered that she had promised certain people to receive communion on their behalf on that very day and she was

devoutly praying that the Lord would impart the gift just described to them as well. She received this reply: 'I grant it to them, but I leave to their own free will when they wish to be arrayed'. And when she asked with what eagerness he wished them to be arrayed, the Lord added, 'At whatever future time, turning towards me a pure heart and entire will, they invoke my grace with even the least word or groan, they will immediately appear in my sight in the same splendid apparel which you have requested for them with your prayers'.

CHAPTER THIRTY-FIVE

THE EFFICACY OF THE BODY OF THE LORD

1. She was also praying the Lord that he should be present to her at the time of her death, that her body's last food might be the life-giving sacrament of the body of Christ. In spirit she received this answer, that in this she had made a request that was not entirely salvific. For the efficacy of that sacrament cannot be diminished by any bodily necessity, therefore much less by that food which a sick man takes against his desire in such painful necessity, only to sustain life to God's praise. And so just as from the reception of that sacrament, through union with which a person is united to God, all that person's good deeds are ennobled, even more so at that time of someone's death after receiving the sacrament all that she does through a pure intention can become meritorious; such things as patience, food, drink and so on, through union with the body of Christ, grow into a vast eternal accumulation of merits.

CHAPTER THIRTY-SIX

THE UTILITY OF FREQUENT COMMUNION

1. Another time, too, when she was about to communicate, she said to the Lord, 'Lord, what are you going to give me?' The Lord replied, 'Myself, wholly and completely, with all my divine power, just as my Virgin Mother received me'. Then she said, 'So what more shall I have than those who received you with me yesterday, and today are omitting to do so, since you always give yourself completely?' The Lord replied, 'If it was the custom among the ancients that he who had twice gained the consulship should take precedence over him who had been recipient of it once, how could it possibly not be that he who has received me more often on earth should not excel much more in glory in eternal life?'

Then groaning she said, 'How greatly will the priests then surpass me in glory, whose duty it is to communicate every day?' The Lord said, 'They will indeed shine with great glory, those who approach worthily; but none the less a disposition of inner joy is far superior to the glory of outward appearance. Thence there is one reward for these who approach from loving desire, but another for those who take with fear and reverence, and yet another for those who are prepared to take with strenuous efforts. But none of these will he receive who only celebrates out of habit'.

CHAPTER THIRTY-SEVEN

THE LORD MAKES AMENDS ON BEHALF OF THE SOUL

1. On a feast of the Blessed Virgin, after receiving special and wonderful gifts, she had come to herself and was thinking over her ingratitude and negligence. Downcast, she was turning over in her mind the fact that, so it seemed to her, she had shown too little reverence to the Mother of the Lord and also to God's other saints, whom she should none the less have glorified very deservedly that very day for the special gift she had received. The Lord soothed her with his usual kindness and said to his most blessed Mother and to the other saints, 'Does it seem to you that I have made you sufficient amends on her behalf, since I have shared myself in the sweetly-flowing pleasure of my divinity with her in the presence of you all?' They replied, 'Truly, this is a far greater amends than was deserved'. Then the Lord gently turned to her soul and said, 'Is this sufficient amends for you?' She replied, 'My Lord, this would be perfectly sufficient for me if only there were not one thing missing, that when you have made amends for my past negligences I immediately add to them future ones, since I am well aware of my tendency to fall'.

The Lord replied to her, 'I shall give myself to you in such a way that I shall make full amends on your behalf not only for your past negligences but also for your future ones. All you have to do is take care that, after receiving the sacrament, you should keep yourself unharmed by the stains of sin'.

And when she replied, 'Alas, Lord, I am afraid that I will not do this very thing as I ought. So please teach me, kindest of teachers, how I can wipe away the stains when I have acquired them'. The Lord replied, 'Never allow them to remain for any length of time in you, but as soon as you realize you are stained immediately say this verse with devout heart: "Have mercy on me, God", or else this: "O my sole salvation, Christ Jesus, grant that through your most saving death all my offenses may be blotted out" '.

Hence when she approached and had received the body of Christ, she realized that her soul was shining like crystal, bright with snowy splendor, and that the divinity of Christ which she had received in herself shone through the crystal like gold miraculously enclosed. And this was performing in her such marvelous and delightful works, beyond what could possibly be imagined, that presented such lovely delights to the ever-to-be-worshipped Trinity and all the saints that she understood this to be what Scripture says: that every spiritual loss can be made up through worthy reception of the body of Christ. For that work of divinity was seen as so surpassingly joyful that all the heavenly court was seen to bear witness to its pleasure in beholding the soul in which these things were being performed.

Also what was written above, that the Lord had promised that he would amend future negligences, must be understood in this way: just as through crystal something which is enclosed appears both from one side and from the other, so[1] through that soul appears that divine operation just mentioned, both when she was intent on the zeal of good works and when out of human frailty she was not intent—except when darkened by clouds of sins, for this alone prevents this most healthful and most truly worthy work in a soul.

[1] Reading *sic* as in the 1885 Solesmes edition, not *si* as in the *Sources Chrétiennes* edition.

CHAPTER THIRTY-EIGHT

THE EFFECT OF THE DIVINE GAZE

1. Having a devotion and frequent desire to receive the body of Christ, one time when she had prepared herself rather devoutly on the preceding days for communion and on the Saturday night felt so weak that it seemed to her that she could not receive communion, as usual she consulted the Lord on what he would rather she did. The Lord kindly replied, 'Just as a bridegroom, satisfied by varied banquets, takes greater pleasure in lingering quietly with his bride in private than in sitting with her at table, so on this occasion I take pleasure in your omitting communion on account of discernment, rather than in your approaching'.

She replied, 'From what, my most loving Lord, do you condescend to declare that you are satisfied?' The Lord replied, 'From every restraint of speech and of all your senses and also from whatever desires, prayers and acts of will on which you concentrated in preparing to receive my most sacred body and blood, I declare that I am satisfied best, as if by the choicest courses of varied banquets'.

2. But when she had come to Mass very weak and was eager for spiritual communion, it happened that the priest who had taken the body of Christ to some sick man came back from the town. Understanding this from the ringing of the bell and inflamed with violent desire she said to the Lord, 'How willingly would I receive you now, life of my soul, spiritually at least, if I had had the time

to prepare myself at all'. The Lord replied, 'The gaze of my divine loving-kindness will prepare you most fittingly'. This done, the Lord seemed to direct his gaze, like the rays of the sun, into her soul, saying, 'I shall fix my eyes on you'.[1] In these words she understood a threefold effect, like the sun, that the divine gaze brings about in the soul, and also a threefold way in which the soul should be prepared to obtain it. For first, the gaze of the divine loving-kindness, like the sun, rendered the soul dazzling white and purified from all stains, whiter than snow.[2] That effect is acquired through humble acknowledgment of one's own faults. Secondly, the gaze of the divine loving-kindness softens the soul and makes it fit it to receive spiritual gifts, just as wax is softened by the heat of the sun and is prepared for imprinting by some seal. This result the soul obtains through devout concentration. Thirdly the gaze of the divine loving-kindness makes fertile the soul with the varied flower of the virtues, just as the sun makes the earth fruitful, to produce different kinds of fruit. This result is obtained through the faithful trust with which a person entrusts her whole self to God and trustingly trusts in the overflow of his loving-kindness, that all things, both favorable and unfavorable, may work together for good.[3]

3. Then, at both Masses when the convent was receiving communion, the Lord manifested himself with such great condescension that he seemed to offer the saving victim with his own worshipful hand to each one as they approached, while the priest none the less was making the sign of the cross over each host. But from each host the Lord Jesus offered to someone, he seemed to give her a very efficacious blessing. She was astonished at this and said, 'Lord, do those who have received you sacramentally just now enjoy a greater result, or I who have freely anticipated so many of your divine blessings?'

The Lord replied, 'Who is considered to be richer? He who is adorned with jewels and precious necklaces, or he who has a

[1] Ps 31:8.

[2] Cf. Ps 50:9.

[3] Rom 8:28.

vast amount of pure gold secretly concealed?' In these words of the Lord she was given to understand that although he who receives communion sacramentally doubtless gains a rich result of salvation, both in body and in soul, according to the faith of the Church, none the less he who omits receiving the body of Christ purely for God's praise, out of the virtue of obedience and of discernment, and communicates spiritually, inflamed by desire and love of God, deserves to obtain just such a blessing of the divine condescension as she herself received at that time. A far more effectual fruit follows in the eyes of God, although this is hidden from human understanding.

CHAPTER THIRTY-NINE

THE USEFULNESS OF REMEMBERING CHRIST'S PASSION

1. With regard to her unworthiness, when one day, the strength of her merits failing as it were, she was lying on the road along which in spirit she was hastening to the Lord, the Lord bent down with his most benevolent loving-kindness and said to her, 'According to the law of marriage, it is appropriate that a king should hasten to see his queen, wherever she has been confined by sickness'. Through these words she understood that the Lord out of his loving-kindness sees himself to be as much bound to the soul that constantly keeps in mind with devotion the remembrance of his Passion as far as she can, as a king is bound to a queen by the law of marriage. For she recognized that she had earned this most courteous visitation of the Lord because she was eager to recall the Lord's Passion on Fridays. She also understood that however lukewarm she became in her devotion, none the less the Lord would always look kindly on her if she did not forget to honor the remembrance of the Passion.

CHAPTER FORTY

HOW THE SON OF GOD CONCILIATES GOD THE FATHER

1. Once she was trying to choose what, among the many things which the Lord out of his generous loving-kindness had condescended to bestow on her from his gifts, would be the most useful to be revealed to people to their benefit. Making his way into her thoughts and desires the Lord gave her this reply: 'It is extremely useful to make known to people that it would be most useful for them always to remember this, namely, that I the Virgin's son stand before God the Father for the salvation of humankind. Whenever they sin in their heart, out of human frailty, I offer my own spotless Heart for them to God the Father in reparation. Indeed, when they sin with their mouth, I hold out my own most innocent mouth; and when they sin with their hands, I show my own pierced hands. And so similarly in whatever they have sinned, my innocence immediately conciliates God the Father, so that when they repent they always win ready pardon. And so as often as my chosen have won the pardon for their sins which they sought I would like them always to thank me because I have brought to pass such ready protection for them'.

CHAPTER FORTY-ONE

THE GAZE OF THE CRUCIFIX

1. One Friday, when the day was already drawing towards evening,[1] she was filled with remorse while gazing at the crucifix. She said to the Lord, 'Ah, my sweetest lover, how greatly and how terribly did you suffer on this day for my salvation! I, most faithless, alas, have held it cheap and have ignored this day, my mind elsewhere, for I have not this day called to mind with devotion that you, my eternal salvation, suffered for me hour by hour, and that you, the life that gives life to all, died for love of my love'.[2]

The Lord answered her from the cross: 'What you have neglected I have made good on your behalf, for hour by hour I have collected into my heart what you ought to have recalled in your heart. Thence my heart has swollen with such great fullness that I awaited with great longing that moment when this intention should be rendered to me from you. And with it, I now desire to offer to God my Father everything that I have made good for you during the day, for without your intention it could not be so salutary for you'. In this, therefore, can be known God's most steadfast love towards a person, a love that makes amends to God

[1] Lk 24:29.

[2] Augustine, *Confessions*, 2.

the Father through that intention alone in which the person realizes that what he has neglected is troublesome to him, and makes good every failing in a most exalted fashion. For this let everyone rightly praise him.

2. Again, when she was handling the image of Christ crucified with devout intention, she understood that if anyone looks upon the image of the cross of Christ with devout intention, she is looked upon by the Lord with such kindly mercy that the soul, like a bright mirror, receives in itself from divine love a delightful image, whence all the court of heaven delights in her. And this shall be her eternal glory in the future, as often as she has done this on earth with affection and due devotion.

3. Another time she perceived this teaching: when a person turns to the crucifix, he should imagine the Lord Jesus saying gently to him in his heart, 'See how, because of my love for you, I hung on the cross naked and despised, my whole body wounded and wracked in every limb. Even now my heart is affected by such sweetness of love for you that if it were necessary for your salvation and you could not otherwise be saved, I would be willing to suffer now, for you alone, all that you could imagine I had ever suffered for the whole world'. By such meditation a person may stimulate his heart to gratitude, for truly one never happens to see a crucifix without God's grace. Therefore it cannot be without guilt that a Christian holds cheap the enormous price paid for his salvation, like an ingrate. For one can never look with intention at the crucifix without fruit.

4. Again, on another occasion her mind was filled with thoughts of the Lord's Passion, and she understood that when someone ruminates on prayers or readings concerning the Lord's Passion, it is far more efficacious than on other themes. For just as it is impossible for anyone to touch flour without getting dusty, so it cannot be that anyone can be intent on the Lord's Passion with even a little devotion without receiving some fruit from it. Also, when one reads anything about the Lord's Passion, at least it makes the soul fit to receive some fruit, in so far as the intention of such a

person who often calls to mind Christ's Passion is more fruitful than the more numerous intentions of another who cares nothing for the Lord's Passion. Therefore let us more often take pains to ruminate frequently on Christ's Passion, so that for us it may become 'honey in the mouth, music in the ear, joy in the heart'.[3]

[3]Bernard of Clairvaux, SC 15.

CHAPTER FORTY-TWO

THE BUNDLE OF MYRRH

1. One night when she had an image of Christ's cross by her bed and the same image was leaning towards her, as if about to fall, she set the image straight and spoke gently: 'Sweetest little Jesus, why are you leaning?' He replied at once, 'The love of my divine Heart draws me to you'. Then catching up that image she laid it gently to her heart, embracing and kissing it, and said, 'My beloved is to me a bundle of myrrh'.[1] Then the Lord, as if taking the words out of her mouth, added, 'He shall dwell between my breasts'.[2] By this means he endowed her with this insight: a person ought carefully to wrap up all the troubles and anxieties of both her heart and body in his own most holy Passion, like someone who inserts a twig in the middle of a bundle. For instance, when worn down by troubles a person is provoked to impatience, let him recall the astonishing patience of the Son of God, who was led to the slaughter for our salvation like a most meek lamb, and did not open his mouth[3] for even a single impatient word. Indeed, when it happens that a person could avenge his anxieties by word or deed, let him take pains to consider again how great was the mildness of heart which led his lover to refrain

[1]Sg 1:12.

[2]Ibid.

[3]Is 53:7.

from paying out evil for evil or avenging himself by a single word. But all that he endured he rewarded most excellently, when by his Passion and death he redeemed those by whom he was persecuted even unto death.[4] Following the Lord's example, let him always take pains to repay good for evil. Again, if anyone is consumed with hatred against those who have harmed him,[5] let him remember that unbounded sweetness by which the most loving Son of God, in the midst of the indescribable sorrows of his Passion and the pains of death, prayed for his crucifiers, saying, 'Father, forgive them'.[6] And in union with that love let him take pains to pray for his enemies.

2. The Lord added, 'Whoever wraps up his own troubles and anxieties, putting them into the bundle of my Passion, and surrounds himself on every side by the example of my Passion in eagerness of imitation, is the one who truly "lingers between my breasts"; so much so that out of special affection I shall grant him, in increase of his merits, all that I have merited through my patience and other virtues'. Then she said, 'My Lord, how do you welcome the fact that some people feel such great affection for the image of your cross?' The Lord said, 'I welcome it with pleasure; but as for those who love my image but do not follow my Passion through imitation, I look on this just as a young girl can welcome from her mother the fact that she dresses her up in various ways to satisfy her own tastes and prestige. She does not do it because the daughter particularly wants it; on the contrary, [the daughter] sometimes strenuously objects. In so far as the mother ignores her wishes, the daughter welcomes the other things lavished on her the less. For she thinks that her mother puts the other ornaments on her to enhance her own prestige and not out of tender affection. Similarly, all the affection and honor and reverence shown to my cross can never seem completely good to me as long as a person does not take pains to imitate the example of my Passion.'[7]

[4] Acts 22:4.

[5] Ps 22:5.

[6] Lk 33:34.

[7] This analogy is somewhat confusing because contrary to what one would expect Christ is comparing himself to the long-suffering daughter, and the imperfect devotee to the mother.

CHAPTER FORTY-THREE

THE IMAGE OF THE CRUCIFIX

1. Sometimes she was very anxious to obtain the image of the holy cross so that she could reverence it more often for love of the Lord. But she was also held back by her conscience because she was afraid that by such a preoccupation she could be hindered from the fruition of God's inner gifts. On this she received this reply from the Lord: 'Do not be afraid, my dearest, for you could not possibly be hindered in spiritual matters because of this, since I alone am the cause of your preoccupation. Also I declare extraordinarily welcome to me the eager devotion by which someone is affected concerning the image of my crucifixion. Sometimes it happens that, because a king often cannot remain with the wife whom he loves tenderly, he leaves one of his dearest relatives in his place with her. Whatever caressing and friendliness the wife shows him, the husband considers as rendered to himself, since he knows that his wife does this not from forbidden love for a stranger but from chaste zeal because of her love for him. In the same way I delight in the reverence shown to my cross, which is done purely for love of me. But not if a person takes pleasure simply in owning a cross, and does not take pains to recall through it the love and faithfulness by which, for his sake, I condescended to undergo the bitterness of my Passion, or if he is in some other way more interested in self-love than eager to imitate the worshipful example of my Passion'.

CHAPTER FORTY-FOUR

HOW THE DIVINE SWEETNESS ATTRACTED HER SOUL

1. One night her mind was devoutly preoccupied with recollection of the Lord's Passion, and as if out of control she was plunged into an abyss of desires. She felt that her liver[1] was greatly inflamed by the excessive heat of her desires and said to the Lord, 'My sweetest lover, if people knew what I now feel, they would say that by rights I should refrain from such fervor, to regain my physical health. But it is clear to you, who know my hidden things,[2] that with every effort of my powers and senses I could not have refrained from the piercing excitement of your sweetness'.

The Lord replied, 'Who in his right mind does not know that the inconceivably powerful sweetness of my divinity exceeds far beyond comprehension all human physical pleasure? Every physical sweetness compared to divine sweetness, is like a tiny drop of dew compared to the vast expanse of the whole ocean. But since people are quite often attracted so powerfully by human pleasure that they are quite incapable of refraining from some of

[1] In the Middle Ages the liver was regarded as the seat of love and violent passion generally, of the soul and of the affections.

[2] Dn 13:42.

them, though they know they will run the risk of eternal danger, not only of the body but also of the soul; how much the less can the soul that is penetrated by the sweetness of my divinity refrain from my love, from which it knows eternal blessedness will come to it?'

2. She said, 'Perhaps they would say that, since I have been professed in a cenobitic order, I am certainly bound to moderate the ardor of my devotion in order to be able to keep the rigor of the Order's rule-governed life'. The Lord condescended to extricate her with this analogy: 'It is as if certain gentlemen of the chamber were appointed to serve assiduously before the king's table in honor of the king, but sometimes the king, afflicted by old age or poor health, would summon one of those standing nearby on whose bosom he delighted to be supported, intending to rest for a while. It would be quite improper if that gentleman of the chamber on whom the king chose to lean were to get up suddenly and let him fall because he had once been appointed to stand before the king's table! Similarly, it is far more incongruous that someone whom in my generous loving-kindness I draw to the enjoyment of contemplation should withdraw from it in order to keep the rigor of the Order of her profession. Since I am the creator and reformer of the whole world, I should take infinitely greater delight in a single loving soul than in all physical labor and exertion that can ever be suffered by someone without love and purity of intention'. And the Lord added, 'But if anyone is not certainly drawn by my spirit to the peace of contemplation and none the less neglects the Order because of his eagerness to acquire contemplation, he seems like someone who without being summoned takes his place at the table with the king, although he was appointed to serve the king at table. Hence just as a servant who takes his place at the king's table without being invited acquires no honor but rather contempt for his lack of respect, so anyone who fails to keep the Order and tries by his own exertion to gain the enjoyment of divine contemplation, which no one can have without my own special gift, sometimes obtains more harm than profit from it: he does not profit in it but grows lukewarm in that to which he is bound. Indeed, anyone who on account of physical convenience

(while he feels there is no necessity present) fails to keep the Rule, seeking external pleasures, acts like someone who, although he had been appointed to serve the king before his table, would go off and disgracefully defile himself by cleaning out the horse stables!'

CHAPTER FORTY-FIVE

HOW THE LORD RECEIVED THE HONOR SHOWN THE CRUCIFIX

1. One Friday, when she had spent a sleepless night on fire with her meditations and desires, she finally remembered with what affection she had drawn the iron nails out of a crucifix which she always had by her, and had replaced them with fragrant gillyflowers. She said to the Lord, 'O sweetest lover, how do you receive that I, having drawn the iron nails out of the sweet-flowing wounds in your hands and feet, have replaced them with affection with sweet-smelling gillyflowers?' The Lord replied, 'I have received that affection to such an extent that in return I have poured into all the wounds of your sins the most noble balm of my divinity. Thence all the saints will take delight eternally in a marvelous way, for your wounds will be pleasing from the infusion of precious liquid'. Then she said, 'My Lord, will you do the same for all who do this?' The Lord replied, 'Not for all, but those who do it with similar affection I shall show similar favor. But those who, inspired by your example, do this with as much devotion as they can, I shall reward adequately though less generously'.

2. Then taking the crucifix and lavishing on it sweet kisses and close embraces she caressed it in many ways. After a while, when she felt weak of heart from her wakefulness, she put aside the crucifix and

said, 'Farewell, my beloved, and good night. Let me sleep to recover my strength which I have completely dissipated in meditation with you'. With these words she turned away from the crucifix as she wanted to sleep. While she was resting the Lord seemed to stretch out his right hand from the cross. Placing it on her neck as if to embrace her and putting his rosy mouth to her ear he said in a charming whisper, 'Hear me, my beloved, for now I shall sing you some sacred love poetry[1]'. And beginning with harmonious voice in the tune to which we sing the hymn 'Christ the King and Creator',[2] he sang this verse:

> May my unceasing love
> Be your continual languor
> May your delicious love
> Be my most welcome pleasure[3].

At the end he said, 'Now, my beloved, instead of the *Kyrie eleison* which is added to each verse of the hymn 'Christ the King', add any request you desire and it shall be granted you'.[4] Then she devoutly prayed for certain causes and they were most kindly granted.

3. After this the Lord again sang that verse and when he had finished he again urged her to pray. In singing the same verse over and over, taking alternate lines, he would not allow her to rest in physical sleep until almost all her strength was exhausted and she had to be refreshed. Finally before day-break she slept a little. But the Lord Jesus who never fails but is always present to those who love him appeared to her during her sleep and gently fostered her in his bosom. It seemed as if he made a most delicious meal for her in the sweetly-flowing wound of his blessed side and with extraordinary

[1] *pro Fescenninis amatoria*, literally 'love poetry in the place of Fescennine verses'. 'Fescennine verses' were ribald Latin wedding-songs.

[2] According to the Solesmes edition, the hymn sung at the end of Lauds with the *Kyrie eleison* during the three days before Easter.

[3] *Jubilus* of the Holy Name of Jesus; PL 184:1318, attributed to Bernard of Clairvaux but probably written by an English Cistercian at the end of the twelfth century. See A. Wilmart, *Le 'Jubilus' dit de Saint Bernard*, Rome, 1944.

[4] Cf. Est 5:3.

fondness he placed each mouthful in her mouth, with his soft hand, to refresh her. Delightfully restored by this in her sleep she awoke and, sensing that she had recovered her strength, gave devout thanks to the Lord.

CHAPTER FORTY-SIX

THE SEVEN HOURS OF THE BLESSED VIRGIN

1. Since one night she had been greatly wearied in keeping vigil and lovingly laboring in mindfulness of the Lord's Passion and had not yet said Matins and sensed that her strength had failed her, she said to the Lord, 'Ah, my Lord, since you know that my human frailty cannot do without rest, teach me what honor or service I could now show your most blessed Mother, since I cannot perform the Hours due to her'. The Lord replied, 'Praise me through my sweet-sounding Heart, in the innocence of the most complete virginity by which she conceived me as Virgin and as Virgin bore me and after the birth remained Virgin inviolate.[1] She imitated my innocence by which, at the hour of Matins, for the redemption of humankind I was captured, bound, struck with buffets and cudgels, and wretchedly and mercilessly inflicted with all sorts of insults and mockeries'. While she was doing this, she saw the Lord offer his divine Heart in the likeness of a golden goblet for his virgin Mother to drink from. After having drunk delightfully of its honeyed sweetness and having been sweetly satisfied, or rather abundantly made drunk and pierced to her very marrow, she was seen to rejoice deliciously.

[1] Antiphon for the Magnificat, First Vespers of the Purification.

2. Then she joined in the praise of the Blessed Virgin, saying, 'I praise you and greet you, Mother of blessings, most worthy sanctuary of the Holy Spirit, through the most sweet Heart of Jesus Christ, most loving Son of God and of you. I pray that in all our needs and at the hour of death you may help us. Amen'. From this she also understood that whenever someone praises the Lord as it is written above, also praising the Blessed Virgin by adding this verse, 'I praise and greet you, Mother of blessings' and so on, it seemed that the most sweet Heart of Jesus Christ her most loving Son was offered to the virgin Mother to drink. The royal Virgin would willingly accept it and in accord with the generosity of her motherly love would kindly reward no matter whom.

3. The Lord added, 'Praise me, in place of Prime, through my sweet-sounding Heart in that most pleasing humility by which the undefiled Virgin was fitted more and more to receive me. She imitated my humility by which I, judge of the living and the dead,[2] at the hour of Prime condescended to stand humbly to be judged before an infidel,[3] for the redemption of humankind'.

4. 'At Terce, praise me in that most ardent desire with which she drew me, the Son of God, from the bosom of the highest Father to her virgin womb. She imitated me in that most ardent desire, with which I desired human salvation when I was struck with hard scourges, crowned with thorns and also at the hour of Terce condescended with great gentleness and patience to carry on my weary and bleeding shoulders the most shameful cross'.

5. 'At Sext, praise me in that most secure hope with which the heavenly Virgin, through her good will and holy intention, always aspired to praise me. She imitated me who, hanging on the lofty tree of the cross, amidst those most bitter pangs of death, longed with all my strength for the redemption of humankind and so I cried, "I thirst". That is, I thirsted for the salvation of the human soul so much so that, if it had been necessary, I would have borne

[2] Acts 10:42.

[3] *Saraceno*, i.e. Pontius Pilate.

still harsher and more bitter pains and would have offered myself as ready to bear all things for human redemption'.

6. 'At None, praise me in that most fervent love shared, that is, between my divine Heart and the undefiled Virgin, which tenderly joined and inseparably united my most excellent divine nature to human nature in the Virgin's womb. She imitated me, the life of the living, at None when on the cross out of my great love I surrendered to most bitter death for human redemption'.

7. 'At Vespers, praise me in that most constant faith by which the Blessed Virgin alone, at the time of my death, when the apostles ran away and all were despairing, stood firm, unmoved in the true faith.[4] She imitated me in that faithfulness by which, already dead and taken down from the cross, I pursued humankind even to the limbo of hell, from which I snatched them with the all-powerful hand of my mercy and transported them to the joys of paradise'.

8. 'At Compline, praise me in that most praiseworthy perseverance by which my sweetest Mother persevered unto the end[5] in all good deeds and virtues. She imitated me, who carried out the task of human redemption with such great care that even after I had won true freedom for humankind by my most bitter death, none the less I did not fail to hand over my incorruptible body for burial in human fashion, to show that I would refuse nothing, however vile, for human salvation'.

[4]Gregory, Homily 25 *in Evangelia*, on Saint Mary Magdalene.

[5]Mt 10:22.

CHAPTER FORTY-SEVEN

DEMONSTRATION OF FRIENDSHIP

1. She was quite often oppressed with great weariness by association with people, as often happens (for to someone who loves God all that is found other than God seems to be inconsolable sorrow); she very frequently used to get up suddenly in fervor of spirit and seek her place of prayer, saying, 'See, my Lord, how all creatures now weary me and I take pleasure only in association and converse with you. So bidding every creature farewell I turn to you, my only and complete good, and the joy of my heart and soul'. And thus kissing the five rosy wounds of the Lord, she would recite this versicle five times: 'Hail, Jesus my spouse, blossoming with the delight of your divinity; I embrace you, greeting you out of affection for all the world, and thus I kiss you on the wound of love'. With these words to the Lord's wounds, as it were, she made all her weariness vanish and was refreshed through the delights of devotion.

2. While she did this quite often, one day she asked the Lord how he welcomed it, since she sometimes concentrated on them [the wounds] for a short time. The Lord replied, 'As often as you turn to me with such an intention, I welcome it as friend would welcome from a friend the fact that he was staying with him for a single day: with ready kindness and wonderful delicacy he would devote to him all the friendship he can demonstrate, both in words, deeds, and also examples. Amidst such proofs of delicacy a guest quite often might

wonder how he could repay his friend fittingly, when he happens to stay with him. In the same way I unceasingly consider in my divine Heart and carefully plan how, in return for the individual occasions you lavish on me on earth, I can repay you in eternity, in accord with the royal liberality of my omnipotence, wisdom and kindness, a hundred thousand times with fondness and friendliness'.

CHAPTER FORTY-EIGHT

THE EFFECTIVENESS OF COMPUNCTION

1. At one time the community feared the appearance of enemies who, it was rumored, were approaching the monastery strongly armed. In the face of this exigency they were chanting the Psalter in common psalm by psalm, with the versicle 'O most blessed light' and the antiphon 'Come Holy Spirit' and she was faithfully concentrating with the others on prayer. She understood in her spirit that through this prayer the Lord was filling the heart of some with compunction by his Holy Spirit, to make them acknowledge their own sins of neglect and repent them with a wish freely to correct them and avoid them in future as far as possible. And when they were thus seized with compunction, she saw emanate from the hearts of each one thus affected by the spirit of compunction something like a vapor that surrounded the cloister and its environs and drove far from them all their enemies. And if someone's heart was greatly filled with compunction and inclined to good will, the vapor coming from her was the more effective in driving further away any opposing force. She understood from this that the Lord was especially intent on drawing the hearts of his chosen community back to him by means of such fear and anxiety of adversaries, so that, shaken by troubles and purified from all their sins of neglect, they would flee to his fatherly protection and would find the more effectively the succor of divine consolation.

2. When she had perceived this she said to the Lord, 'Why, most loving Lord, are those things that you condescend by your generous loving-kindness to reveal to me quite frequently so different from the revelations of others that as a result it quite often happens that other people notice them, although I would rather conceal than publish them?' The Lord replied: 'If some teacher were questioned by large numbers of people speaking different languages and were to reply to them all in one language only, it would not be useful nor accepted by everyone. But if he answered everyone according to the interpretation of their own language, speaking to a Latin-speaker in Latin, a Greek-speaker in Greek, the more he answered each one appropriately in his own language, the more discriminating his wisdom would prove to be. In the same way the more differently I communicate my gifts to anyone, the more brightly shines the unsearchable depth of my wisdom by which I answer everyone in a way appropriate to their understanding. I reveal what I want, according to a person's intellectual capacity with which I have endowed him, that is, by showing things to the more simple through largely physical analogies, and to the more intellectually capable by expounding more hidden and obscure shadowy sketches'.

CHAPTER FORTY-NINE

THE PRAYER THAT PLEASES THE LORD

1. Another time when on account of the same exigency the psalm 'Bless [the Lord, my soul]'[1] was being recited by the convent, with the set prayers after each verse, she was taking her part very devoutly with the others. The Lord appeared to her as if all beautiful and lovely, and at each verse, when the convent, prostrate on the ground, was asking forgiveness, he raised his left arm as if to greet her and offered her the most sweet wound in his most holy side to kiss. While she kissed it repeatedly, the Lord showed that he welcomed this astonishingly. Then she said to the Lord: 'Since I perceive that you, my most loving Lord, are so affectionately delighted with this, I ask you to teach me some short prayer that your loving-kindness will welcome with similar honor, whoever offers it devoutly'. Then divinely inspired she understood that if anyone with devout intention says these three verses five times, that is: 'Jesus, savior of the world, to whom nothing is impossible save only not to have mercy on wretches, hearken to us', and 'Christ, who redeemed the world by your cross, hear us', and 'Hail, Jesus my spouse, sweet as honey with the delight of your godhead, greeting you with the whole world's love I embrace you and so kiss you on the wound of love', and 'Lord, my strength and my praise, you are

[1]Ps. 102/103 or 103/104.

my salvation'[2] and so on in honor of the five wounds to God and, kissing devoutly the Lord's rosy wounds, would add any collects or prayers they like, and would commend through these the sweetest heart of Jesus Christ, the mouthpiece[3] of the Holy Trinity; the Lord would condescend to accept this in place of a prayer, however laboriously composed.

2. Again, another time when the same psalm was being repeated, the Lord Jesus appeared to send out as it were burning flames towards God the Father for the community, as if from the wounds of a crucifix which was as usual raised up before the community. He was showing in some sort the uncontrollable nature of the most burning desire and love by which his heart was moved towards God the Father, for the salvation of the community.

[2] Ps 117:14 and Is 12:2.

[3] *organum*.

CHAPTER FIFTY

THE DELIGHT OF THE LORD'S SENSES IN HER SOUL

1. Overtaken by sickness one day when about to receive communion, she realized that her strength had completely failed and that consequently she could experience less devotion. She said to the Lord: 'Oh sweetness of my soul, since (alas!) I know only too well that I am unworthy to receive your most holy body and blood, if I could find alleviation or pleasure in any creature apart from you I would not receive holy communion this time. But since from east to west and from south to north I can call to mind absolutely nothing in which I could delight and experience refreshment of body and soul alike other than in you; therefore ardently panting, sighing and running in the thirst of my desires I come to you, the living fountain'.

The Lord, according to his kindness, courteously accepted this and repaying her the same loving compliment in return answered: 'Just as you affirm certainly that you can take no pleasure in any creature apart from me, so I too confirm in my divine power that I never wish to take pleasure in any creature apart from you'.

2. But while she was pondering in her heart the fact that, although the Lord condescended out of his kindness to say that he did not wish to take pleasure in any creature apart from her, none the less

this could change at some time; the Lord made his way into her thoughts and replied: 'For me, to wish is the same thing as to be able; and so "I can" is no different from "I wish" '.

She replied: 'And what, oh most courteous lover, can you find in me, the dregs[1] of creation, in which you could take any pleasure?' The Lord replied: 'The gaze of my divinity takes pleasure in a manner beyond human understanding in looking upon you, whom I created, in your many and various gifts of my graces, so acceptable to me in every way. My divine hearing too is affected as if by the most delightful musical instruments in all and from all the words of your mouth with which you cajole me, whether praying for sinners or for souls in purgatory, whether correcting some people, or teaching, or offering some word in whatever way to my praise. Even if no further profit results in someone from this, none the less from your good will and intention directed at me it echoes with a sweet sound in my ears and moves to the depths the inmost being of my divine Heart. Also your hope, by which you sigh for me, exhales the delight of a most pleasing perfume to my sense of smell. All your groans and desires, too, taste sweeter to me than all spices.[2] Your love, too, offers me the pleasure of a most delightful embrace'.

3. Then she began to long for the Lord to condescend to restore her to her original state of health as soon as possible, for this purpose, that she could follow the rigor of the Order more devoutly. The Lord kindly replied to her: 'Why would my bride want to be a nuisance to me, by going against my will?' She replied: 'Lord, surely you do not judge this desire of mine to be against you? It seems to me that I am clearly seeking nothing but your praise in this'. The Lord replied: 'I am pretending not to hear your speech on that subject, as if it were girlish chatter; but if you were to insist more importunately, I would not welcome it'. She understood from these words of the Lord that anyone who longs to be healthy solely in order to serve God, does well indeed But it is far more perfect for a person to entrust himself completely to the divine will, in full trust that whatever fate God ordains for him, whether better or worse, is the most healthy for that individual.

[1] 1 Cor 4:13.

[2] Sg 4:10.

CHAPTER FIFTY-ONE

THE HEARTBEATS OF THE LORD JESUS

1. When she saw others hurrying off to a sermon, she plaintively said to the Lord: 'You know, most loving one, that right now I would be heartily glad to hear a sermon, if I were not prevented by sickness'. The Lord replied: 'Do you wish me to preach to you, dearest?' She replied, 'Very, very much'. Then the Lord let her lie on his Heart, so that the heart of her soul was placed next to his divine Heart. When her soul had taken sweet rest there for a while, she felt in the Lord's Heart two wonderful and intensely delightful beats. The Lord said to her: 'Each of those two heartbeats works human salvation in three ways. The first beat works the salvation of sinners; the second, of the righteous. For by the first beat in the first way I continuously address God the Father, winning his favor for sinners and inclining him to mercy. Secondly, I address all my saints, excusing a sinner in their eyes with brotherly faithfulness and inspiring them to pray for a sinner. Thirdly, I address the sinner himself, mercifully recalling him to penitence and awaiting with unspeakable desire his conversion.'

2. 'With the second beat in the first way I address God the Father so that he must rejoice with me that the ransom of my blood was paid out so profitably for the redemption of the righteous, in whose hearts I now delight to take such varied pleasure. Secondly, I address all the heavenly host so that we may together praise the

praiseworthy way of life of the righteous and that they must thank me for all the blessings that have been given[1] and will from now on be given. Thirdly, I address the righteous themselves, coaxing them to salvation in many different ways and faithfully urging them that they may go forward from day to day, from hour to hour.[2] And just as the human heartbeat is not hindered from constantly beating by sight or hearing or any manual labor, so the government and disposition of heaven, of earth, or of the whole universe can never, even a little, slow or modify or hinder in any way these two beats in my divine Heart, even unto the end of the world'.

[1] Prayer of Thanksgiving.

[2] Ritual of Baptism.

CHAPTER FIFTY-TWO

HOW THE LORD WELCOMES A FRIEND'S[1] RESTLESSNESS

1. After this she had spent one almost entirely sleepless night that had made her so weak that she was now bereft of all her strength. In her usual fashion she offered the Lord this lack of her strength to his everlasting praise, for the salvation of the whole world. The Lord kindly took pity on her and taught her to call upon him with these words:

2. 'By the most tranquil delight with which you lay from eternity in the bosom of God the Father, and by your most lovely stay in the virginal womb, in which you rested for nine months in your Mother's womb; by the most joyful pleasure with which you have ever condescended to take delight in some loving soul: I ask you, most merciful God, not for my own comfort but for your eternal praise, to condescend to grant me a little rest by which my body's weary limbs may be restored to full use'.

3. And while she was saying these words, it seemed to her that by them she was approaching the Lord, as if by climbing stairs. Then the Lord showed her a truly lovely resting-place prepared at his right

[1] *amici*, omitted by the Solesmes edition.

hand, saying to her: 'Come, my chosen one, repose above my Heart and prove whether my restless love may allow you to rest'. And when she had thus reclined above the honey-sweet Heart of the Lord and was experiencing its most delightful heartbeats quite powerfully, she said to the Lord: 'Sweetest lover, what are those heartbeats saying to me?' The Lord replied: 'I am saying this: whenever someone exhausted by wakefulness for me and bereft of strength asks me, through those three clauses that I inspired you to say, that I should grant him rest to my praise and to restore his strength, and I have not hearkened to his prayer; if then he humbly bears with his weakness, by embracing patience,[2] my divine delight and kindness welcome this from him the more delightfully. If a friend rouses his special friend, who was sound asleep, from a delightful dream, purely and simply because he would take pleasure in chatting with him, and he [the friend] were promptly to get up to satisfy his pleasure and to put himself out a great deal, he would welcome it more than if another of his friends who usually stays awake all night should serve both their interests, that is those of his own as well as of his friend's. For it is infinitely more welcome to me when someone, after his strength has been exhausted in vigil, humbly and patiently bears with his weakness in his sickness and offers it to me, than when someone in physical health stays awake the whole night in prayer with good results'.

[2]RB 7.35, Fourth degree of humility.

CHAPTER FIFTY-THREE

THE LORD GOD'S PLEASURE

1. When she was sick, the fever would sometimes reduce after sweating and sometimes grow worse. So one night when she was damp with sweat she began to worry whether her sickness would take a turn for the better or for the worse as a result. The Lord Jesus appeared to her, all lovely like a flower, bearing health in his right hand and sickness in his left. He offered her both hands for her to choose which she would rather desire. But she spurned both and, dashing between the Lord's hands in fervor of spirit, fled to that sweetest Heart in which she knew lay concealed abundance of all good, searching to know what was his most praiseworthy will. Receiving her courteously and gently embracing her the Lord laid her to rest on his Heart. But she immediately turned her face away from the Lord and resting the back of her head on the Lord's breast, said: 'Look, Lord, now I am turning my face away from you, for it is my whole-hearted desire that you should pay no attention to my will but should carry out your good and most praiseworthy pleasure in all that concerns me'.

2. (Through this it can be observed that a faithful soul commits itself and all its affairs with such sure trust to divine disposal that it would even take delight in not knowing what the Lord is doing about it, so that he may perfect in it the more purely what is pleasing to his

divine will.) Then the Lord sent forth from both sides of his sweet-flowing Heart, as if from a cask with its spigots fully opened, two streams that flowed into her bosom, saying: 'Because in completely renouncing your own will you have turned away your face from me like this,[1] I send out and direct to you all the sweetness and pleasure of my divine Heart'. She replied to this: 'Since you, my sweetest lover, have so often given me your deified Heart in various ways, I should like to know what fruit I ought now to seek, in that you again grant it me so freely'. He replied: 'Does not the catholic faith hold that anyone who receives communion on a single occasion, to him I give myself for his salvation with all the benefits contained in the treasuries of my divine and human natures alike? And the more often, however, a person has received communion, the more greatly the accumulation of his blessedness is increased and multiplied'.

[1] Ps. 29:8.

CHAPTER FIFTY-FOUR

SENSUAL DELIGHT IN GOD

1. When she was advised by a number of people to refrain from contemplation until she recovered her former good health, she had greater faith, in her usual fashion, in others' opinion than in her own. Acquiescing to their advice, she made this agreement, that she be allowed more external delights in decorating the images of Christ's cross, so that she might be distracted by such games from her inner eagerness for contemplation and none the less through the external representation of Christ's image could have a continual awareness of her only love. Consequently one night she was busy thinking how she would prepare a delightful sepulcher out of cloth for her crucifix, in which she would hide it on Friday at Vespers in memory of the Lord's Passion. The kindly Lord, who pays more heed to the intention than to the action of one who loves him, involved himself in this occupation and said to her: ' "Delight in the Lord", dearest, "and he will give you the requests of your heart" '.[1] In these words she understood that when someone, for God's sake, seeks delights in such activities, then the Lord takes delight in that person's heart, just as the head of a household takes delight in the merriment of a minstrel at his feast when [the minstrel] himself takes delight in his own performance. And this is the heart's request

[1] Ps. 36:4.

that is granted to a person who thus innocently takes delight in more external things for God's sake, for the human heart naturally requests—that is, desires—God to delight in him.

2. Then she said: 'And what, most loving God, can you have from such delight, that serves the senses rather than the spirit?' The Lord replied: 'Just as a greedy money lender would unwillingly neglect the opportunity to earn a single penny, so I who have decided to have pleasure in you would much more unwillingly allow a single thought or movement of your little finger, done for my sake, to come to nothing, because I did not turn it to the advantage of my great praise and your eternal salvation'.

She replied: 'If your vast goodness condescends to take such great delight in these things, how much delight, then, you must take in that song to your praise that I have composed from the sayings of the saints, in which your whole worshipful Passion is commemorated'.

The Lord replied: 'Just as someone would take delight in the fact that amidst tender embraces his friend would lead him into a most lovely garden where the most delightful scent of a gentle breeze wafts its way to him, and would take wonderful delight in the welcome blossoming of varied flowers, and would be ravished by the soothing harmony of most delicious music and refreshed by the sweetest savor of the finest fruit; so I shall repay you with just this very delight, and also anyone who devoutly repeats that song on that narrow path that leads to eternal life'.[2]

[2]Mt 7:14.

CHAPTER FIFTY-FIVE

LOVESICKNESS

1. A little while after this, when confined to bed for the seventh time she was meditating one night on the Lord, he himself bent towards her with a most courteous caress and said: 'My beloved, declare that you are sick with love for me'.[1] She replied: 'How could I, unworthy as I am, presume to say, "I am sick with love for you"?' The Lord replied: 'Everyone who spontaneously offers his own will to suffer some burden for my sake can truly take pride in that and in taking pride can declare to me that he is sick with love for me, while he perseveres in suffering the burden and keeping his mind fixed on me'.

Then she said: 'What could you gain from such a declaration, most loving Lord?' The Lord replied: 'Such a declaration is the delight of my divine nature, the honor of my human nature, the loveliness of my eyes, the praise of my ears'. And the Lord added: 'That messenger who bears the declaration will receive abundant consolation. In addition, the unction of my love is aroused so powerfully that it violently compels me to heal the contrite of heart, that is, those who long for grace; to preach to the prisoners, that is, forgiveness to sinners; liberation to the captives,[2] that is, redemption to the souls in purgatory'.

[1]Sg 5:8.

[2]Is 61:1 and Lk 4:18–19.

2. Then she said to the Lord: 'Father of mercies, are you not finally condescending after this seventh sickness to restore me to my former state of health?' The Lord replied: 'If I had let you know in your first sickness that you would have to take to your bed seven times, you would perhaps have trembled from human weakness and fallen into impatience. In the same way if I were to promise you that this was the last sickness you would have to endure, you would certainly concentrate hopefully on its end, and thence your merit would be diminished. And so the fatherly foresight of my uncreated wisdom profitably arranges that you remain ignorant of both, so that you are always compelled to yearn for me with all your heart and to commit to me all your troubles, both outer and inner, with whole-hearted confidence. I look on you with such sweet faithfulness and am concerned for you, so I certainly do not allow you to be burdened more than you can bear,[3] since I am well aware of the tenderness of your delicate patience. You can certainly consider this, that after your first sickness you felt greater weakness than you are now experiencing in this seventh one. Although human reason judges this to be impossible, nevertheless my divine omnipotence can perform it.'

[3] 1 Cor 10:13.

CHAPTER FIFTY-SIX

THE REASON FOR HER INDIFFERENCE TO LIFE AND DEATH

1. One night while she was caressing the Lord in many ways, among others she asked why it was that, although she had by now been sick for some time, none the less she had had no desire to know whether her sickness would end in death or recovery, but rather death and life were all the same to her. The Lord replied: 'When a bridegroom is taking his bride to a rose garden where he may collect rose blossoms to weave a garland for him, the bride takes such great pleasure in her husband's sweet conversation that she never asks what kind of roses her husband wants to gather. But when they have reached the rose garden, then whatever rose the bridegroom has picked and given his bride for weaving into a garland, the bride weaves it promptly and eagerly, without any discrimination. In the same way, a faithful soul whose highest joy is my will and who takes delight in it as in a rose garden certainly welcomes it as all the same whether it is my pleasure to restore her to health or to put an end to this present life. For she undoubtedly entrusts herself with complete faith to my fatherly care'.

CHAPTER FIFTY-SEVEN

HOW THE DEVIL WAS TERRIFIED AT HER DISCERNING REFRESHMENT

1. Another night, when she had been greatly weakened by the many consolations of the Lord's presence and the stress of spiritual insights, taking grapes she refreshed herself, with this intention, as if she were restoring the Lord himself within her. The Lord magnanimously welcomed this and said to her: 'I confess that in this way reparation has been made to me for that bitterness I drank from the sponge on the cross for love of you, since I now suck in its place indescribable sweetness from your heart. And the more you refresh your body purely to my praise, the more sweetly I confess myself restored in your soul'.

2. But when she collected the grape skins and seeds in her hand and threw them into the middle of the room, Satan, the enemy of all that is good, was there.[1] He tried to gather up what she had thrown away, as evidence of the sick woman's guilt in having eaten before Matins, contrary to the religious life. He had scarcely touched one of the bits of skin with a couple of fingers when he was consumed by a fire of unbearable torture. Letting out terrible shrieks he bounded out of the room, taking the greatest care not to let his feet touch any more bits, from contact with which he had experienced the torture of such unbearable pain.

[1]Jb 1:6.

CHAPTER FIFTY-EIGHT

THE USEFULNESS OF FAILINGS

1. One night while scrutinizing her heart she acknowledged a failing in it, namely that she was often accustomed to say out of habit, 'God knows!' without intention or necessity. Reproaching herself for this she desired from the Lord that he should completely correct this failing in her and grant her this as a gift, never to take in vain his honey-sweet name. The kind Lord fondly replied: 'And why would you want to deprive me of that honor and cheat yourself of an infinite reward that you earn every time you acknowledge this failing or one like it, and determine to avoid it in future? For whenever someone is eager to overcome his failings for love of me, he shows me as much honor and fealty as a knight would show his lord if vigorously engaging in battle against his enemies he bravely were to attack them all with main force and lay them low'.

2. Then, when it seemed to her that she was resting in the Lord's bosom and she felt a great failing in her heart, she said to the Lord: 'Look, most loving Lord, I offer you my feeble heart with all my emotions and inclinations, for you to take delight in according to your every good pleasure'. The Lord replied, 'I welcome your feeble heart offered me with such love more graciously than another's strong heart; just as an animal that has been much hunted is more welcomed than a domestic animal, because its flesh is more tender and delicious to eat!'

CHAPTER FIFTY-NINE

COMFORT IMPOSED BY THE LORD

1. When she could not attend choir because of sickness, she still used to go quite often to hear the Hours so as thus to exert her body in God's service. When she considered that she had not concentrated on God with as careful devotion as she desired, she often bewailed this to the Lord, saying with dejection of spirit: 'My most loving Lord, what honor do you now have from my sitting here negligent and useless, concentrating with difficulty on one or two words or notes?' Finally the Lord replied on one occasion: 'And what would you have if, on one or two occasions, your friend were to offer you a draught of very sweet fresh mead that you hoped would greatly fortify you? You should know then that I have much greater delight in the individual words and notes on which you concentrate to my praise.'

2. During Mass, when she was reluctant to stand for the gospel, her strength failing, she was arguing with herself over this for she did not know what profit there was in such prudence, if she were to spare herself this task, as she did not expect to recover her former health. As usual she asked the Lord what would be praiseworthy to him. The Lord replied: 'When you perform with difficulty something that is beyond your capacity for my praise, I welcome it from you just as if I had needed it for the profit of my honor. But when you omit such tasks and admit physical comforts, still

concentrating on me, I welcome this too as if I myself were sick and could not do without that particular comfort. And so either way I shall reward you in proportion to the glory of my divine magnanimity'.

CHAPTER SIXTY

THE RENEWAL OF THE SACRAMENTS

1. She was scrutinizing her heart one day and discovered something that she would willingly have confessed. Since she could not have a confessor she fled as usual to her only solace, the Lord Jesus Christ. Lamenting, she explained the impediment to him. The Lord replied to her: 'Why are you distressed,[1] beloved? For whenever you desire something from me, I the high priest and true bishop will be with you and on each occasion I shall renew in your soul all seven sacraments at once, more potently than any priest or bishop could do on seven separate occasions. For I shall baptize you with my precious blood; I shall confirm you in the strength of my victory; I shall espouse you to me in the faith of my love;[2] I shall consecrate you in the perfection of my most holy way of life; I shall absolve you[3] from every chain of sin in the loving-kindness of my mercy; I shall feed you with myself in the overflow of my love and I shall be filled with my enjoyment of you; and I shall pierce with such potent unction all your inner being in the delight of my spirit that through all your senses and emotions I shall be distilled as a succulent source[4] of devotion. Then you will be prepared for eternal life and sanctified without ceasing.'

[1]Lk 24:38.

[2]Hos 2:20.

[3]Absolution, Third Nocturn.

[4]*adeps*, literally 'fat, suet, lard'.

CHAPTER SIXTY-ONE

THE EFFECTIVENESS OF CHARITY

1. Another time while very weak she had got up for Matins and had just completed one nocturn, when another sick sister had come by with whom she had, in charity, read Matins a second time with much difficulty and trouble. During Mass, while she was concentrating devoutly on the Lord, she realized that her soul was honorably adorned with wonderful garments and marvelously glittering precious stones.[1] Divinely taught, she understood that she had earned such adornment because, in charity, she had humbly read for a second time with a younger sister the part of Matins already read, and thence she was shining with as many jewels as the words she had re-read.

Then, mindful of certain negligences that she had not yet confessed, because her confessor's absence had prevented it, with sorrowful voice she laid this before the Lord. The Lord replied: 'And why do you complain of your negligences, you who are so gloriously enveloped in a cloak of charity that covers a multitude of sins?[2]' She replied: 'And how can I find consolation in the fact that charity covers my faults, by which I none the less recognize that I am stained?' The Lord said: 'Charity not only covers sins, but rather like the heat of the sun it consumes and eradicates all negligences of venial sins and in addition confers an accumulation of merits'.

[1] Second response of the office of Saint Agnes.

[2] 1 Pt 4:8.

CHAPTER SIXTY-TWO

THE PROMOTION OF THE RELIGIOUS LIFE

1. Once she saw a person acting rather carelessly as regards certain observances of the Rule. She feared she would incur guilt in the sight of God if, although she knew, she failed to reveal it. At the same time out of human frailty she was afraid that some of the more easygoing sisters would say she was more concerned than was necessary in revealing minor matters. In her usual fashion she offered this to the Lord for his eternal praise. The kindly Lord showed that he welcomed this with joy and said: 'As often as you endure this characterization,[1] or a similar one, for love of me, I shall defend you most strongly and I shall build around you on every side a fortification from all cares that can in any way keep you from me, just as by analogy a city is fortified with ramparts and wall. In addition I shall add to the accumulation of your merits every merit that anyone can earn if she humbly were to obey your advice with devout zeal, to my praise'.

[1] *verbum*.

CHAPTER SIXTY-THREE

THE LORD'S FAITHFULNESS TOWARDS THE SOUL

1. It generally happens that a person takes injuries inflicted by a friend more seriously than by an enemy, according to the text, 'For if my enemy had cursed me' and so on.[1] So when she had understood that someone for whose salvation she had shown greater eagerness and faithfulness was not responding to her with the faithfulness she owed but rather was turning upside down, as if in scorn, certain things bestowed on her by [Gertrud], she was distressed and sought refuge in the Lord. The Lord kindly comforted her, saying: 'Do not be sad, daughter, for I have allowed these things for your greater health. For I, taking great pleasure in your companionship and constant company, so that I could enjoy them more often, am like a mother who has a little boy whom she loves so dearly that she wants him to be with her all the time; when the boy wants to run off to his friends because of a secret game, she sometimes puts scarecrows or something terrifying in certain areas so that the frightened boy runs back to her bosom. So I, wishing you never to be absent from my side, allow your friends to thwart you in something. Thus when you find no complete faithfulness in any creature you may run back

[1] Ps 54:13.

to me all the more eagerly as you realize that there is more reliable abundance of all delights and faithfulness in me'.

2. Then the Lord caught her up like a delicate child into his bosom. He caressed her in many ways, putting his divine mouth next to her ear and soothing her in various ways. He said: 'Just as a kindly mother is accustomed to kiss fondly anything that troubles her delicate child, so I desire to soothe away by the blandishments of loving whispers all your troubles and contrarieties'. And when she had been delighted in the Lord's bosom for some time in many ways by the infinite caresses of divine consolations, the Lord offered her his Heart, saying: 'Now look into the innermost reaches of my Heart, my beloved, and ponder carefully how faithfully I have disposed and adorned for the most profitable and healthy benefit of your soul all that you have ever directed at me; and consider whether you could accuse me by a single word of unfaithfulness!'

When she had done this, the Lord seemed to her to be constantly adorning her with the same trouble mentioned earlier as if with marvelously shining golden flowers. Then, remembering certain women whom she knew to be burdened by other troubles, she said to the Lord: 'How much more than me do they deserve to be compensated by your loving-kindness with more worthy reward and to be adorned with more precious ornaments, merciful Father. For they are suffering such burdensome troubles and are not relieved by any such consolations as relieve me. I am, alas, completely unworthy for I am very often supported and do not however put up with such things as happen to me with worthy patience'. The Lord replied, 'In this as in all things I show towards you the delicate care of most tender love. Just as a mother who loves her little child would gladly adorn him with gold and silver, but knows he cannot bear the weight of the ornament and adorns him with more fragile flowers that pour out splendor but do not weigh him down, so I too moderate your troubles, lest you should give way under their weight, and none the less you do not lose the merit of patience'.

3. Then considering the depth of the divine loving-kindness for her salvation, out of great gratitude she broke into devout praises.

Then she understood that those ornaments that had been previously shown her for her trouble like fragile but glorious flowers, were being rendered more solid through that gratitude that had prompted her to sing praises to God for her adversity. From this she understood that that grace God had given to enable her to praise him in her adversities was supplementing more nobly the weight of her troubles, just as an ornament of pure gold is more precious than one of silver that is gilded only on the surface.

CHAPTER SIXTY-FOUR

THE FRUIT OF GOOD WILL

1. A knightly delegation had come to the convent to take some people from our community to set up the religious life in another monastery and word of this had reached her. Because of her excellent will and her prompt attention to all that pleased God, although bereft of physical strength she was spurred on by her zeal for divine praise, and before a crucifix offered God her heart in fervor of spirit to his eternal praise, for the perfecting of all his good pleasure in body and soul. The Lord appeared so profoundly pleased at this offering that, coming down from the gibbet of the cross as if with great joy and most loving fondness, he caught her up in most delicious embraces, exulting beyond our powers of description. Just like a sick man who, having already completely abandoned hope, rejoices at the offer of a long desired and hoped-for medicine that he hopes will fully restore him to his former state of health, he laid her gently to the wound in his most holy side and said: 'Welcome, my dearest, as the most gentle plaster for my wounds and the sweetest alleviation of all my sufferings'. She understood in these words that when someone offers up his entire will to God's good pleasure, whatever trouble he knows threatens him, the Lord welcomes this just as if that person at the time of his Passion had laid the gentlest of plasters to all his wounds.

2. Persisting in this prayer in her heart she was making very many plans in which, if it should fall to her lot that she should go out [to make the new foundation], she would be willing to promote and uphold the praise of God and increase of the religious life, as far as she could. Meanwhile, various thoughts made their way into her heart and finally, coming to herself, she reproached herself with having wasted so much time thinking to no purpose of things from which perhaps no result would follow, since she herself was so weak that she seemed to be approaching death rather than departure [for a new foundation]. Moreover if it ought to be, she would have plenty of time for making plans about such matters.

Then the Lord Jesus appeared to her, as if in the midst of her soul, in great glory, surrounded by the blooms of roses and lilies.[1] He said to her: 'Pay attention to how I am glorified from the disposition of your good will, as if with the splendors of sparkling stars and golden candelabra, just as we read that John, in the Apocalypse, saw one like the Son of Man in the midst of golden candelabra, holding seven stars in his right hand.[2] And I am affected by the rest of your varied thoughts that came into your heart as by the loveliness and delight together of fresh roses and lilies'.

3. Then she said: 'Ah, God of my heart,[3] why do you perplex my mind with so many varied inclinations that come to nothing? For a few days ago you persuaded my mind and aroused my desire for hastening the sacrament of Extreme Unction; while I was preoccupied in many ways about that, you gladdened me with many consolations in addition. And now, on the contrary, you provoke my desire to establish the religious life somewhere else, although I am still so unwell that I could hardly walk the necessary distance!' The Lord replied: 'Indeed I tell you that, as I said before at the beginning of this book,[4] I have planned to set you as a light for the gentiles,[5] that

[1] First response of the feast of the Assumption; Si 50:8.

[2] Rv 1:13–16.

[3] Ps 72:26.

[4] I.Prologue.3.

[5] Is 49:6; cf. Is 42:6.

is, as a source of light for many, it is necessary that different people should find in your book different things suited to them for their own instruction and consolation. Also it often pleases friends to chat to one another about many things from which no result follows. And also a friend sometimes plans difficult things with his friend so that by this he may test in a certain way his friend's faithfulness towards him, and welcomes wholeheartedly the kindly intention of his good will towards him. In the same way I too take delight to make plans with my chosen about various things that never actually happen, to test their love and faithfulness towards me and so that I may reward them for an unlimited number of things that they could never actually carry out, for I regard every inclination of theirs as if it were carried out. I also inspired your mind with a desire for death and so for a hastening of Extreme Unction. And so all things that your devotion, both in will and in deed, has accomplished in preparing for such things I have put aside for you in the depths of my divine Heart for eternal salvation. So you must know what is said: "If the righteous man is surprised by death, he will rest in peace";[6] if it happened that by some accident you were surprised by sudden death or were not able to receive Extreme Unction when fully conscious, as very often happens to my chosen, you will suffer absolutely no disadvantage from this. For all those preparations for death that you had made some years ago stay fresh and green in the unfading freshness of my eternity, thanks to the power of my divine cooperation, and are producing for you the fruit of eternal salvation'.

[6] Ws 4:7.

CHAPTER SIXTY-FIVE

WHAT ZEALOUS ACTIONS WIN BENEFITS

1. At someone's request she was offering the Lord all those things his freely-given loving-kindness had condescended to perform in her, that they might give way to the salvation of the one who was requesting it. At once that person for whom she was praying appeared standing before the Lord, sitting on his throne of glory. He had on his lap a marvelously embroidered garment that he spread before her, but in which he did not dress her. Much astonished at this she said to the Lord: 'A few days before at a similar offering of mine you transported the soul of that poor little person for whom I was then praying to lofty joys of heaven without delay. Why then, most kindly God, from those same benefits of yours bestowed on me, totally undeserving as I am, do you not adorn her, who urgently wishes it, with this garment that you spread before her?' The Lord replied: 'When some offering is made me in charity for the souls of the faithful departed, out of my vast loving-kindness I whose nature is always to spare and have mercy[1] take pity on their need, since I know that they can help themselves no further in any way. At once I give them what is offered on their behalf as remedy of absolution or relief, or as increase of eternal blessedness, according

[1] Prayer for the Dead.

to their state and their merit. But when similar offerings are made me for the living, I certainly put them aside for their salvation, but since they can still augment their own salvation themselves with good works, desire and a virtuous will, it is right that they should be zealous by their own efforts to further what they long to gain from the merits of others'.

2. 'And so, if the woman for whom you are praying longs to be adorned with a cloak of benefits bestowed by me, let her be zealous in spirit for three goals. First, let her stoop with humility and thankfulness to take up the cloak, that is, let her humbly confess that she is in need of others' merits and let her return me loving thanks that I condescend to make up her need through others' abundance. Secondly, let her lift up that cloak with hope and trust, that is, by hoping in my goodness let her trust that she will gain great profit of salvation from me in her soul. Thirdly, let her put on the cloak by laboring in love and in the other virtues. And let anyone do the same who longs to share in the benefits of others and the merits of their virtues. Then she will be able to gain profit from them'.

3. Once when she had been bled before Lent these words often came to her: 'O most excellent King of kings, most illustrious prince', and others of the same sort. When she had recollected herself early one morning in a place of prayer, she said to the Lord: 'Most loving Lord, what do you wish to become of these words that so often come into my mind and spring to my lips?' Holding in his hand a golden necklace made from four parts, he showed it to her. While she was wondering what the four parts denoted, she was taught by divine inspiration that Christ's divinity was symbolized by the first part, Christ's soul by the second part, the faithful soul whom he has betrothed with his own blood by the third part, and Christ's spotless body by the fourth part. Also the fact that she saw in this necklace the faithful soul set between Christ's soul and his body gave her to understand the indissoluble cement of love with which the Lord fixes the faithful soul to his own body and soul. And suddenly by looking at this necklace she was inspired with these words by powerful energy:

You, my soul's life,
May the love of my heart
Be made one with you,
Fused with strength of loving heat.
In all to which it turns without you
Let it be left lifeless.

For you are the charm of every color,
Sweetness of every savor,
Fragrance of every scent,
Delight of every sound,
Delicious charm
Of close embraces.

In you delicious pleasure,
From you rich superabundance,
To you charming allure,
Through you loving influence.

You: overflow of godhead's abyss,
O King of kings most worthy,
Emperor most excelling,
Prince most illustrious,
Ruler most mild,
Defender most strong.

You: life-giving jewel of human nobility,
Craftsman most skillful,
Teacher most gentle,
Councilor most wise,
Helper most kind,
Friend most faithful.

You: savory union of intimate delight,
O caresser most delicate,
Paramour most mild,
Lover most ardent,
Spouse most sweet,
Zealot most chaste.

You: flowering blossom of prime beauty,
O brother most lovable,
Youth most gorgeous,
Comrade most joyous,
Host most generous,
Servant most courtly.

I set you above all creatures;
For you I renounce every pleasure,
For you I meet every hardship,
In all these I seek your praise alone.
You the quickener of these and every good
I declare with heart and voice.

In the strength of your fervor
I unite my devotion's intention
To the power of your prayer
That through the integrity of divine union
I may be led to the summit of perfection,
Every rebel impulse consumed.

4. Each phrase gleamed like brilliant jewels worked into the golden necklace.

The next Sunday following, while she was at Mass, about to communicate, and was reciting those words most devoutly, she saw the Lord taking delight in them. She said to him: 'Most loving God, since I feel how much you delight in these words, I wish to counsel as many other people as I can to offer you the same song, in their prayers, like a necklace'. The Lord replied: 'No one gives me what belongs to me! But if anyone recites those words devoutly, I shall increase in her the grace of my knowledge and she will receive in herself the splendor of my godhead to shine in her through the potency of those words, just as someone who holds pure gold up to the radiant sun, in that it is gold, sees the light reflected in it'. She soon felt the effect of these words and when she had finished that prayer, the face of her soul appeared lit up more brightly by the radiance of the divine light and, so it seemed to her, she received with greater relish the taste of divine thought.

We would like to add here some things that seem the more profitable, which God revealed to her when she was praying for certain people.

CHAPTER SIXTY-SIX

THAT THROUGH HER THE LORD INFUSED STREAMS OF GRACE

1. Once the Lord Jesus appeared to her asking her for her heart, saying: 'Give me your heart, beloved'.[1] When she gladly did so, it seemed to her that the Lord laid it to his own divine Heart like a water-pipe and thus reached the earth. By this means he spread the streams of his boundless loving-kindness far and wide, saying: 'Look, from now on I always take delight to use your heart as a water pipe. Through it I may pour out to all who work to receive the pressure of that infusion, that is, who with humility and trust ask you for the broad streams of divine consolation from the honey-sweet torrent of my Heart'. The gracious effect of these words will, in part, become clear in what follows.

[1] Prv 23:26.

CHAPTER SIXTY-SEVEN

HUMILITY UNDER GOD'S SCOURGING

1. One day she was praying for certain persons who had damaged the monastery by despoiling it and were in addition oppressing it excessively. The kind and merciful Lord showed himself to her as if he were suffering from one arm so far bent back that it was almost torn out of its socket. The Lord said: 'Consider what pain would torment me if someone were now to punch me on that arm. Judge that I am burdened with a similar pain by all those who, with no pity for the damnation of souls risked by those who attack my own people, wickedly proclaim over and over again those people's failings and the injuries inflicted on themselves, not remembering that those people too are my members. Indeed all those who, moved by compassionate mercy, beg for my clemency, that I should mercifully turn them from their error to a better life, soothe[1] my arm as with most gentle ointments. But those who kindly guide them to reconciliation and amendment by counsel and advice are like thoroughly experienced doctors who gently re-set my arm into its proper place by manipulation'.

2. Then astonished at the Lord's indescribable kindness, she said: 'By what judgment, most merciful God, can people who are so unworthy be called your "arm"?' The Lord said: 'Because they are

[1] *deliniunt*, from *delinio*, *delenio*.

from the body of the Church, whose Head I am proud to be'. But she said: 'Right now, my Lord, see how they are unfortunately cut off from the body of the Church by an interdict, for they have been excommunicated and publicly denounced because of the damage they inflicted on our monastery'. The Lord replied: 'All the same, as they can still make their peace with the Church through reconciliation, constrained by my own loving-kindness, caring for them I long with incredible desire that they should turn to me through penitence'.

Then she prayed that he would condescend to guard the community with his fatherly protection from their assaults. The Lord replied: 'If you all are humbled beneath my powerful hand,[2] acknowledging before me in your hearts that you deserve to be punished as your negligences demand, my fatherly mercy will keep you unscathed from every attack of your enemies. But if through pride you all become wickedly arrogant towards those who besiege you, hoping or praying that they will receive evil in return for evil, my justice and my just judgment will allow them to prevail against you, harming you and troubling you in very many ways'.

[2]Pt 5:6.

CHAPTER SIXTY-EIGHT

THE ACCEPTABILITY OF EXTERIOR WORKS

1. One year the community was in great distress because of a debt and this woman was devoutly intent on praying the Lord in his loving-kindness to move the stewards of the convent to pay off what they owed. The Lord, gently soothing her, replied: 'What profit would I gain from it if I helped them in this?' She replied: 'They would have time to engage more zealously and devoutly in spiritual exercises'. The Lord said: 'And what good does that do me? I have no need of your good works[1] and it makes no difference to me whether you have time for spiritual concerns or are sweating away at exterior works, as long as your will is directed at me with free intention. For if I took pleasure in spiritual exercises only, I would have immediately reconstructed human nature after the Fall so that from then on it would not need food or clothing or the other things for which human industry sweats, in seeking out and putting together the necessities of life. But just as a powerful emperor not only takes pleasure in having refined and elegant girls in his palace, but also appoints princes, dukes, knights and other servants fit for various tasks, each one of whom he has constantly available in his palace for his varied affairs; so I too not only take pleasure in the

[1]Ps 15:2.

interior delights of contemplatives, but also in the varied tasks of practical business that is done for the sake of my honor and love. I am drawn to linger and dwell delightfully among the sons of men, for they labor greatly in such works, in love, patience, humility and the other virtues'.

2. Then she saw the man on whom the greater responsibility lay, sitting in the presence of the Lord, as it were leaning on his left side. Raising himself awkwardly over and over again, he offered the Lord with his left hand, on which he was leaning, a gold coin distinguished with a precious stone. The Lord said to her: 'Look: if I were to lighten the burden on him for whom you pray, then I would lose that noble jewel that pleases me in that coin. He too would be cheated of his reward, for then he would only offer me with his right hand a coin without the jewel. For he offers simply a coin if, without adversity but still in accordance with the divine will, he is intent on God in all his deeds. But he offers God a gold coin with a most excellent stone if he is dogged by adversity in all that he does, and still does not quarrel with the divine will'.

3. When she did not give up, but prayed the Lord more urgently to lighten that burden on the convent's stewards, the Lord replied: 'Why does it seem hard to you if someone endures burdens for my sake, since I am that one true friend in whom faithfulness never grows old? For when a person draws near the end, bereft of all human help and comfort, if someone then remembers some faithfulness shown by him, he does so with great bitterness. But I, the one true friend, come to the comfortless soul at that time of anxious need with a bouquet of all the good works that person ever performed in thought, word, or deed in this life. They are all flourishing like roses and lilies in my garments. And from that the flourishing vigor of my divine presence revives the soul to the hope of eternal life;[2] for it realizes that it is summoned to it and is rewarded for each separate deed. And then the soul, through its pleasure, assumes the ability by which it can, once released from the flesh, receive eternal happiness so that truly rejoicing and breaking

[2]Ti 1:2.

out into praise it can say that verse from Genesis, "Behold the smell of my beloved is like the smell of a fertile field".[3] For just as the body consists of various limbs joined together, so the soul consists of emotions, which are fear, sorrow, joy, love, hope, hate and shame. In so far as a person exerts himself to my praise in each of these, he finds in me joy that cannot be fathomed or described and the pleasure of security by which he is prepared and fitted for eternal blessedness. For in the resurrection to come, when this mortal body will put on incorruptibility,[4] then every individual human limb will receive the individual reward of its deserts, for every single labor and exertion carried out in my name and for love of me. But the soul will receive the nobility of an incomparably more worthy excellence for every single exertion of holy emotions by which the soul was ever moved for love of me, or pierced with compunction, or that invigorated the body'.

4. Then, again feeling compassion for a faithful steward of the convent, she earnestly prayed the Lord that he would mercifully make up to him for the difficult labors he often performed in the community's affairs. The Lord replied: 'The body of that man, which is so often battered for my sake by such labors, is to me like a treasure chest in which I place as many silver coins as the number of times he has moved a limb to obtain necessities for those in his charge. His heart is to me like an ark in which I rejoice at having as many gold coins hidden as the number of times, motivated by his thoughts, he made careful provision, to my praise, for his subordinates'.

Then she said to the Lord with astonishment: 'Lord, that man does not seem to me so perfect that all his acts have been undertaken purely for your praise. But I believe that often other reasons motivate him, such as worldly profit, and consequently physical comfort. And how then could you, my God of unadulterated sweetness, have such delight as you claim in his heart and body?'

The Lord replied very courteously: 'Because his will is so conformed to my divine will that I am always the supreme cause

[3] Gn 27:27.

[4] 1 Cor 15:53.

for all his actions. Therefore in each one of his thoughts, words and deeds he reaps a priceless harvest. But if he concentrated on each of his affairs with a purer and more devout intention, then all his affairs and deeds would be as much the more noble as gold is worth more than silver. Similarly if he concentrated with purer and more devout intention in directing each of his thoughts and preoccupations at me, then they would be as much the more noble as the finest gold[5] and most highly refined is better than old and tarnished gold'.

[5]Sg 5:11.

CHAPTER SIXTY-NINE

THE REWARD OF PATIENCE

1. It happened on one occasion that a person was accidentally injured while working and was suffering great pain. Feeling compassion for her, this woman was praying to the Lord for her, that he would not allow a member, injured in a righteous work, to be endangered. The Lord kindly replied: 'She will certainly not be endangered, but will purchase a matchless reward for this suffering. Also all the members that are moved to serve that member to relieve her pain and cure it will similarly gain an eternal reward from it, just as when one piece of cloth is being dyed with saffron, if something else falls in it is dyed the same. And so when one member suffers,[1] all the other members that serve it will be rewarded together with it by eternal glory'.

2. Then she said: 'My Lord, how can members deserve so great a reward for serving each other, since they do this not so that the wounded member may suffer more extensively or patiently for your love, but only for this, to relieve her suffering?' The Lord gave her a reply of inestimable consolation, saying: 'I have sanctified that suffering that a person bears patiently for love of me which, after the usual remedy for pain, he cannot assuage by his own effort,

[1] 1 Cor 12:26.

in those words with which I prayed to the Father in the extreme moment of my need, saying: "Father, if it were possible, let this cup pass from me",[2] that a person may garner incomparable reward and merit through it.'

3. She replied: 'Does it not please you more, my God, that someone should patiently suffer for your love whatever befalls her than what she is suffering at this moment, when it can by no means be avoided?' The Lord replied: 'This lies hidden in the abyss of my divine judgments and transcends all human understanding; but according to what can be discerned by human judgment, the difference between the two is like that between two exquisite colors, both of which are judged by people to be of such great beauty that it is difficult to discern which should be preferred to the other'. Then she desired of the Lord that he should give that person powerful consolation in these words, as they had been unfolded to her. The Lord replied: 'No. But you should know that I disregard this by the hidden dispensation of my divine wisdom: that is, so that the person herself may be tested further and particularly may be commended in three virtues, that is, patience, faith and humility. In patience, for if she felt such power of consolation from these words as now you sense, every burden of hers would be lightened, so much so that the reward of her patience would also be lessened. In faith, so that she may trust more in another for what she herself does not feel; for, according to Gregory, faith has no reward if human reason offers proof.[3] In humility, so that she may trust that another is superior to her in that he knows, through divine inspiration, what she is not worthy to know'.

[2]Cf. Mt 26:39.

[3]Gregory the Great, Homily 26, as quoted in Lection XII for the Octave of Easter.

CHAPTER SEVENTY

PROFESSION OF GOD'S BENEFITS

1. She was praying for a certain person, sorrowing because she had heard her say something impatiently, that is, why did God send her such troubles, which were inappropriate to her? The Lord said to her: 'Ask that person what troubles are appropriate to her and tell her that since it is not possible to win the kingdom of heaven without any trouble, let her now choose for herself what seems suitable for her and, when these have come her way, then let her practice patience!' In these words of the Lord she understood that the most dangerous kind of impatience is this, when it seems to someone that she would be very patient in other circumstances but cannot in those that the Lord sends. On the contrary, a person ought always to have faith that what the Lord sends is more useful, and when she fails to practice patience in that situation she should be humbled by that.

2. The Lord also added, as a loving endearment, 'And what do you think about yourself? Do I not send you, too, unsuitable burdens?' She replied: 'Not at all, my Lord. But I confess, and will confess it as long as I am able to draw breath, that both in body and in soul, both in good fortune and in bad, you have provided for me in the most suitable fashion that never could any wisdom have exceeded it, from the beginning till the end of the world, except you, sole

Wisdom uncreated, my most sweet God, "reaching from end to end and strongly and sweetly ordering all things" '.[1]

3. Then the Son, gently catching her up, took her to God the Father, asking her to make profession to him. Then she said: 'I give you thanks, holy Father, as far as I can, through him who sits at your right hand, that I have received such magnificent gifts from your generosity. For I confidently recognize that no power could ever have exceeded this, except only for your divine power that invigorates and rules all created things with strength'.

From there he led her to the Holy Spirit, that she might make profession to his goodness. Then she said: 'I give you thanks, dear Spirit Paraclete, through him who became human by your cooperation in the virgin womb, that you have in all things gone so gently before me, unworthy though I am, in the blessings of your freely-given sweetness.[2] For I am sure no kindness would ever have done so, except only for your unspeakable sweetness, in which lies hidden, from which proceeds, and with which at the same moment is received every good thing'.

4. Then the Son of God, embracing her most lovingly and kissing her, said: 'Therefore after this profession I take you into my special care, above every care that I owe to anyone by right of creation, of redemption, and of special election'. From this she understood that when someone makes similar profession to the divine goodness, entrusting and committing herself with thankfulness to his providence, then the Lord takes him into his special care, just as a superior is obliged to take greater care of his subject, after his profession.

[1] Ws 8:1.

[2] Ps 20:4.

CHAPTER SEVENTY-ONE

THE EFFICACY OF PETITION

1. Another time she was praying for those entrusted to her and remembering one person before others with greater affection she said to the Lord: 'Hear me, kindest Lord, according to the sweetness of your fatherly affection, when I pray for her'. The Lord replied: 'I do hear you often, whenever you pray for her'. She said: 'Why then does she call on me so many times with such hesitant words, as if she never receives any comfort from you but is always conscious of her own worthlessness?' The Lord replied: 'This is my bride's most fastidious demeanor, with which most of all she provokes my affection for her, and her most elegant apparel in which she is pleasing to me, that she should be dissatisfied with her own state. And the more you pray for her, the more this increases'.

2. Similarly, another time when she was praying for her together with another, the Lord replied: 'I have drawn them closer to me; hence it is very necessary that they should be purified by troubles, like a favorite daughter who, because of her tender love for her mother, wants to sit on a seat as high as her mother but must sit less comfortably than the other daughters, who choose their own seats near their mother. Nor could the mother's fond glance be aimed at her as directly as at those who sit opposite her'.

CHAPTER SEVENTY-TWO

THE SUCCESS OF PRAYER

1. One time, when about to pray for many people and for various concerns with which she had been entrusted, she flung herself devoutly at the feet of the Lord Jesus and with burning desire pressed most potent kisses on those most saving wounds as devoutly as she could, while she commended to the Lord the people and concerns that had been entrusted to her. While she was doing this she saw what looked like a little stream springing from the Heart of the Son of God himself and copiously overflowing wholly round about.[1] From this she understood that through that little stream the Lord poured out to her all the effects of the petitions that she had entrusted to him at his feet. She said to the Lord: 'My Lord, what good then does it do those for whom I prayed, since they themselves are not aware of the effect of my requests, and so do not believe nor gain any comfort from it?'

The Lord provided this comparison: 'When a king declares peace after a lengthy war, this cannot be known immediately by those who are far away, until it is announced to them at the appropriate time. In the same way those who are rather far away from me through lack of faith or other failings cannot be aware when someone is praying for them'.

[1]Jb 10:8.

2. But she said: 'Lord, there are others among those for whom I prayed just now who I know on your authority are not far from you'. The Lord replied: 'You are right. But all the same if there were someone to whom the king wished to make his decisions known, not through a messenger but in person, he would have to wait until the time seemed opportune to the king. Similarly I determine to make known in person the result of your prayers, at the time most opportune for them'.

3. Then, when she was praying in particular for someone who had once harmed her, she received this reply: 'It is impossible for someone's foot to be pierced without his own heart suffering with it. In the same way it is utterly impossible for my fatherly loving-kindness not to look with effects of compassion on one who, although he realizes that, burdened by his own aberrations, he needs the healing power of divine forgiveness, is guided by the affection of charity and does not fail to make supplication for the salvation of his neighbors'.

4. Since it is human to pray more often for the sick, once when she was about to pray for a particular sick person she asked the Lord what he would particularly like her to pray for on his behalf. The Lord replied: 'Just say two prayers for him with devout heart. First, pray that I may preserve his patience. Second, pray that every moment during which he is to suffer I may lead him to more welcome praise of me and to more useful profit for the sick man's salvation'. And the Lord added: 'As often as you repeat these words, you increase both your own merit and that of the sick man, just as when a painter paints over a picture he intensifies the original color'.

5. Similarly, she was praying for certain office holders and understood that quite often the Lord took greater pleasure in those office holders who held the status of prelate, in that although they had it, they were as those that had not;[2] that is, they exercised the power of prelature as if it had been granted them for a day or an hour, and were always ready to give it up at any moment. However, they

[2] 1 Cor 7:29.

were often concerned about the usefulness of their work, how they could to the best of their abilities gain the greatest praise for God. It is as if they are always saying in their heart: 'Come on, hurry! Do not fail to do this for God's praise, and then gladly lay aside the burden of office when you have performed to the best of your ability everything that you know is a source of praise for God and of use for your neighbor'.

6. She was also praying for someone who had, both through intermediaries and in person, commended himself to her prayers with great humility and devotion. She saw the Lord leaning towards him with the greatest condescension, surrounding him completely with a glory of heavenly light, and with that light graciously pouring out all that he hoped he could obtain through the merit of her prayers. And thus she was instructed by the Lord that whenever someone entrusts himself to the prayers of another, in complete trust that he can win divine grace through that person's merits, the kindly Lord unhesitatingly blesses him according to his desire and his faith, even if the person to whom he has entrusted himself fails to pray devoutly for him.

CHAPTER SEVENTY-THREE

CONCERNING VARIOUS MEMBERS OF ONE RELIGIOUS ORDER

1. When she was praying for a person who had a strong desire, she received this reply: 'Tell him from me that if he desires to be joined with me in union of intimate love, he should strive, like the noble bird,[1] to build himself a nest at my feet from the twigs of his own worthlessness and the branches of my worthiness. Let him rest there in the continuous recollection of his own worthlessness, for mortal man left to himself is always prone to evil[2] and slow to good, unless my grace goes before him. Let him also frequently ponder my mercy, calling to mind with what fatherly love I am ready to receive someone who turns to me in penitence after a lapse. When he wants to fly away from the nest for food, let him come to my bosom where he may call to mind, in loving gratitude, the varied benefits that I generously bestow on him out of the superabundance of my loving-kindness. But if, by spreading the wings of his desire even further, he takes pleasure in aspiring to greater heights, let him soar like the swift eagle above himself through the contemplation of heavenly things. Flying towards my face, borne up on the wings

[1] That is, the eagle.

[2] Gn 8:21.

of the seraphim by the daring of love, let him see the king in his beauty[3] with the eyes of the mind'.

2. 'But since it is impossible in this life to remain for long on the summit of contemplation,' (which according to Bernard is here obtained with difficulty, rarely, and fleetingly), 'let him fold his wings again mindful of his own worthlessness and immediately descend to his nest and there let him wait a while until he once more delights to fly away through thanksgiving, seeking charming food, and consequently as if in ecstasy of mind let him attain the heights of divine contemplation. And thus constantly alternating between these states, either going in through consideration of his own frailty, or going out through reception of benefits, or soaring through contemplation of heavenly things, let him always find the delights of heavenly joys'.

3. Mindful of someone who had been devoutly entrusted to her, who, renouncing the world after the flower of his youthful prime had been consumed, had vowed himself henceforward to the Lord, to serve him in the habit of religion, the handmaid to the Lord showed him her heart. It was her desire that, according to what he had promised her, as is clear from what has gone before,[4] he should be willing to pour out, as if through a water-pipe, the blessings of his divine consolations on anyone who humbly asked her help, and also that he would condescend to fulfill this to his own high praise and to the comfort and profit of the person mentioned. At once she saw her heart set up like a water-pipe and placed against the honey-sweet Heart of most loving Jesus, the Son of God, who appeared to her sitting on his royal throne.

4. Then she saw that person for whom she was praying approaching and reverently kneeling before the Lord. The Lord kindly stretched out his left hand to her and said: 'I shall take him to my incomprehensible omnipotence and unsearchable wisdom and most sweet kindness'. At these words the Lord was seen to offer that person

[3]Is 33:17.

[4]See III.66.

three fingers of his left hand, that is, the index, the middle and the ring fingers. That person, in his turn, placed the same fingers of his own left hand exactly on top, that is, his ring finger on the Lord's ring finger, his middle finger on the middle finger and his index finger on the Lord's. They fitted beautifully. When this was done the Lord turned over his blessed hand so that the fingers of the person already mentioned appeared to be underneath and his own above. Through this he led her to understand three ways in which that much-mentioned person ought to strive to conduct his way of life:

5. First, that whenever he wanted to undertake some task, he should always, with lowliness of heart, try to fit in with the divine omnipotence, by confessing that he is an unprofitable servant,[5] as one who had unprofitably consumed the vigor of his youth, giving little thought to the Lord God, creator and lover. He should desire and pray that out of his divine omnipotence God would grant him the strength to act virtuously.

Secondly, that he should declare to the unsearchable wisdom of God that he is unworthy to receive the infusion of divine knowledge, because he has not trained his senses from childhood to strive for divine things but more often he used them for human vanity, or for vainglory. Thus let him plunge into the deepest valley of humility and strain every nerve to free himself from all earthly concerns and be free for divine contemplation. And from those things with which he superabounds from the overflow of divine generosity, let him strive to share in love with his neighbors as time and place permit.

Thirdly, that he should welcome with the greatest thanksgiving the fact that out of his generous loving-kindness the Lord has given him a good will, through which the two preceding actions are performed.

6. She also saw that the Lord had a little ring on his left hand of some base metal, that had a most noble stone of fiery red. She understood from this that the ring symbolized the worthless way of life of the person previously mentioned, which he had offered to God when

[5] Lk 17:10.

he renounced the world and vowed that he would do battle for the Lord.[6] But the jewel symbolized the loving-kindness of the divine generosity that disposes the Lord, from the lavish loving-kindness of his divine generosity, to infuse a good will, by which all his actions are made perfect in the sight of God. And so the cry, that is, the intention, of that person should be nothing other than praise and thanksgiving for such a most courteous gift of the divine generosity. She also understood that whenever that person accomplished some good will with God's help, the Lord immediately placed it on his right hand, like a precious ring, displaying him as if boasting of this to all the heavenly host, because he has received such a present[7] from his bride (that is, from that person's soul). This excites all the citizens of heaven and they feel as great affection for that person as ever princes can feel more affectionately towards their king's betrothed. For they declare that they are bound by as great a bond of fealty and affection as princes should rightly show towards their lord's chosen bride. And whatever help the Church already triumphant in heaven can and ought to show the Church still militant on earth, all this she grants him at every moment, whenever they have been excited in the way already mentioned by God.

7. Similarly, when praying more devoutly for another person she perceived this instruction, according to which he should conduct his whole way of life: he should build his nest in the hollow places of the wall[8] in the most holy side of the Lord Jesus and lingering deep in the tunnels he should suck honey from the rock,[9] that is, sweetness of intention from the deifying Heart of Jesus. And thus following what he can most carefully find on the way of life of Christ in Holy Scripture he should strive to imitate all its examples, and especially in three things.

The first of these is, that the Lord quite often spent the whole night in prayer[10] and as a result he too should always flee to the

[6]RB, Prologue.

[7]*xenium*: cf. Si 20:31.

[8]Sg. 2:14.

[9]Dt 32:13.

[10]Lk 6:12.

refuge of prayer in all his trials and tribulations. Secondly, that just as the Lord went around the cities and towns preaching[11] so he should strive, not only in word, but also in every deed, gesture or any movement of his body, to edify his neighbor through example. Thirdly, that just as Christ the Lord dispensed varied benefits to the needy, so he should with his own words and actions dispense this benefit: that whenever he plans to say or do something, he should always precede action with the intention to commend it to the Lord in union with his most perfect actions, according to his most laudable will, ordering it for the salvation of the world. After completion, let him again offer that in the same union to the Son of God for him to correct and present worthily to God the Father for eternal praise.

8. She also understood that whenever that person wanted to leave that nest, he should use three supports, stepping on one of them and borne up by one on the right and another on the left. The first support must be devout charity, that would gladly draw to God all men and women, in God's charity, as far as is possible for them, and would gladly be of use to everyone, for God's praise, in union with that love by which the Lord worked the common salvation of the entire human race. Let the second support, that is, the one he should use on the right, be humble subservience, by which he is humbly subjected[12] to everyone for the sake of God; and above all, he should be careful lest someone, either above or below him, should be scandalized at his words or deeds. The third support, that is to bear him up on the left, ought to be careful watchfulness, that is, that he may watch to keep himself completely safe by his greatest efforts, lest he should ever contract some stain by his thoughts, words or deeds, from which he could incur even the slightest divine displeasure.

9. She was also praying for someone else and was shown the condition of his way of life in this way: for he appeared before the throne of God building a magnificent throne for himself out of

[11] Mt 9:35.
[12] 1 Pt 2:13.

square-cut jewels, and was using as it were pure gold for cement. And sometimes he sat down and rested on the throne that he was building, and sometimes he got up and was again hard at work building that throne higher. From this she understood that the jewels symbolized various troubles that preserved and ennobled God's gift in that man's soul. For the Lord makes the path of his chosen difficult in this life, lest while they might take pleasure along the path they might forget those things that exist in their native land. The gold that joined the jewels together denoted the spiritual grace he possessed with which he had to cement together all his trials and tribulations, both inner and outer, for the advancement of his salvation with full and sure trust. The fact that he sometimes sat down and rested on that throne showed that sometimes he took pleasure in the enjoyment of divine consolation. But the fact that he got up again and went on building denoted the continuous repetition of the practice of good works, by which that man made progress from day to day and raised himself up towards perfection.

10. While she was praying for another person, his state was revealed to her in this way. She saw a most beautiful tree before the throne of glory of the divine majesty. Its trunk and branches were blooming with lovely green growth, but its leaves were glowing with golden splendor. The person for whom she was praying was climbing this tree and as it were cutting off with some kind of tool some little branches that were just beginning to wither. When he had cut these off, he was immediately offered another branch from the throne of God, who seemed surrounded on every side by branches of the same color. He grafted this in place of those that had been cut off. As soon as it was inserted it grew strong and seemed to produce reddish fruit that he gathered and offered to the Lord, and the Lord took extraordinary pleasure in it.

11. The tree denoted the religious life that the man, for whom she was praying, had entered to serve God. The golden leaves denoted the good works he was performing in the Order that, by the merits of a relative of his, who had led him to the Order and had entrusted him to the Lord with devout desires and prayers, were counted so much the more worthy as gold surpasses other metals. The tool with

which he cut off the withered branches denoted the consideration of his own failings, which he acknowledged and cut off through worthy penance. The branch that was offered him from the throne of God to graft in place of the twig that had been cut off, symbolized the perfection of the most holy way of life of Jesus Christ that, at the intercession of the merits of the relative mentioned earlier, always compensates more readily for his failings. The fruit that he gathered and offered the Lord symbolized the good will that he possessed to correct his failings, in which the Lord greatly delighted. For he finds much more welcome the good will of a sincere heart than great works without purity of intention.

12. After this, while she was praying for two people who had been devoutly entrusted to her but of whose condition she knew nothing, she said to the Lord: 'You, Lord, who know the hearts of all people,[13] condescend to reveal to me, though I am very unworthy, some things about these two that are pleasing to your will and consonant with their salvation'. Then the Lord very kindly set before her two revelations that had been granted her a little before, concerning two other people for whom she had been praying at the time. One of them was learned but the other was unlearned; the latter was however as devout as the former. The Lord said that he set out the same revelations made about those people for the instruction of these. And he added: 'By the five earlier revelations and these two following ones, anyone of whatever religious order or profession could find some instruction that is appropriate to him'.

13. The revelation made about the condition of the person mentioned, that is, the one who was learned, was such: for when she was praying for her, the Lord replied: 'I have caught her up with the Apostles to the mount of enlightenment. Hence let that person strive to conduct her way of life according to the interpretation of the names of the apostles who went up on the mountain. Accordingly Peter is interpreted as 'he who knows'. Therefore let her strive in all the writings she reads, to search with careful reflection to know

[13] Acts 1:24.

herself. For instance, when she reads something about the vices or[14] virtues, let her carefully ponder whether she can still find any of the vices in herself, and how far she is herself making progress in those virtues. And so in knowing herself more perfectly let her strive also according to the interpretation of the name of James, which means 'one who trips up another's heels',[15] to overthrow in manly conflict every vice in herself and faithfully try for proficiency in the virtues she lacks. But since John means 'in whom is grace', let her strive every day for at least one hour between day and night, in the morning or in the evening or whenever it seems particularly good for her, to withdraw from all outward distractions and recollect herself, so as to be free for me and to see what is my will. And whatever I shall inspire in her at that time, whether to praise me or thank me for my benefits, those bestowed both on her and on all the world, or to pray for sinners or souls in purgatory, let her then exert herself in this with the greatest devotion she can command, during the time which she has set herself'.

14. The revelation concerning the unlearned person was this: she was depressed because she seemed to be prevented from prayer by the various cares of the office entrusted to her. And so when [Gertrud] was praying for her she received this reply from the Lord: 'I have not chosen her so that she should serve me only at one hour of the day, but rather that she should be with me all day long without any respite: that is, she should do all her work unceasingly to my praise, with the intention with which she would like to pray. And let her add this devotion, that is, that in all the work in which she toils in the course of duty, let her always desire that those who make use of her labors should be not only refreshed in body but should also be drawn in spirit to my love, and strengthened in all good. And whenever she does this, it seems to me that she seasons well each of the dishes of her work and labor with the strongest salt'.

14 reading *siue* for *sine*; the 1875 Solesmes edition reads *vel* here.

15 Jerome, Ep. 69.6.

CHAPTER SEVENTY-FOUR

THAT THE CHURCH IS SYMBOLIZED BY CHRIST'S MEMBERS

1. Similarly, while she was praying for a certain person the King of glory, the Lord Jesus Christ, appeared to her, who showed himself to her in the form of his own body, the mystical body of the Church, whose bridegroom and head[1] he condescends to be called and to be. He was seen on the right side solemnly distinguished with royal garments but on the left side of his body naked and entirely full of sores.[2] From this she understood that the Lord's right side represented certain chosen ones in the Church who by the gift of special grace and by the merits of virtues were anticipated by the Lord in the blessings of sweetness;[3] but the left side symbolized certain imperfect souls who still have their faults. The regalia with which the Lord's right side appeared adorned denoted those services and benefits that some people, out of special devotion, strive to lavish on those whom they acknowledge as more distinguished than others by the special privilege of their virtues or the grace of divine intimacy. For whenever someone benefits God's chosen for the sake

[1]Eph 4:15.
[2]Lk 16:20.
[3]Ps 20:4.

of the grace conferred on them by God, it seems that the right side of the Lord is adorned with a new ornament.

But there are some who gladly benefit good people for God's sake but, criticizing the failings of the bad or imperfect more harshly, sometimes harm through impatience rather than correct. These people seem to batter the Lord's sores furiously with their fists, and from those sores corrupted matter, expelled by the sudden assault, seems to fly out in their faces (that is, of the critics), infecting them and contaminating them. But the kindly Lord, overcome by his own loving-kindness and stimulated by the love of his special friends whom they benefit, pretends to ignore all this and gazes on the ornaments of the benefits lavished on his special friends and wipes away those stains with his right-hand garment, that is, for the sake of the merits of his chosen.

2. And the Lord added: 'Would that some people at least would condescend to learn further by means of the squeezing out of their friends' sores how they could cure the sores on my body, namely the Church, that is, the failings of their neighbors: first by handling them gently—that is, by gentle reproaches made in love—let them strive to correct their neighbors' failings. When they consider that they can make no progress in this way, as time goes on let them strive to heal by reproving more harshly. But there are some who do not seem to care about my sores—namely, those who know of their neighbors' failings and even despise them as a result, but none the less are too busy to correct them, even by a single word, lest perhaps they might themselves incur some inconvenience, deceiving themselves by repeating with Cain the threadbare excuse: 'Am I my brother's keeper?'[4] These people seem to apply to my wounds a dressing that does not heal but rather makes my wound go rotten and crawl as it were with worms while by their silence they allow their neighbors' failings to increase, although they could perhaps have corrected them with a few words'.

3. 'There are also some who, while they publish their neighbors' failings for the sake of correcting them, if they do not immediately

[4] Gn 4:9.

see that they corrected or judged them to their own liking, constantly become irritated and decide indignantly in their heart that in future they will not benefit or correct anyone, since it seems to them that no one pays any attention to what they say. But none the less they do not stop criticizing their neighbors quite harshly in their own heart, and sometimes they even blacken with slanders; and none the less they do not utter any word of advice or correction. Those people too seem to put a dressing on my sores that covers the outer swelling after a fashion, but inside it torments as if painfully lacerating my sores with a fiery pitchfork'.

4. 'Those who could correct, even though they pass up the opportunity not maliciously but just uncaringly, seem as it were to trample on my feet. For those who, carrying out their own will according to their liking, do not care that one of my chosen causes scandal, just as long as they satisfy their own pleasure, seem as if by seizing my hands they are piercing them horribly with fiery hooks'.

5. 'Similarly there are also others who love with genuine affection[5] superiors who are perfect and devout and, as is right, honor and praise them with both words and deeds. But they somehow despise their overbearing[6] and imperfect superiors and, judging with impatient heart more severely, they scorn all their actions. These people seem to adorn the right side of my head beautifully, as if with precious stones and pearls, but the left side of my head, the ulcerated side, that I long to lean on them for resting, they seem to reject cruelly and moreover attack it with merciless blows. There are also others who praise extravagantly the misdeeds of their prelates or superiors, so that by gaining their friendship in this way they may be allowed the more freely to serve their own will. These people truly seem to bend my head painfully backwards, and by contemptuously scoffing at my pain, take some sort of pleasure in the worms on my head'.

[5]RB 72.10.
[6]1 Pt 2:18.

6. Since, then, through this revelation the Lord Jesus seems to make the Church his own in this way, as if the good were the right side of his body but the worse the left side, any Christian ought to be especially alert as to how he should exercise ministry to the healthy or the sick body of Christ. For it would seem utterly abominable if someone were to torment his friend's sores with blows, or treat them with poisoned dressings, or spurn his head when it was resting on him, or force it backwards. Similarly everyone should mentally abhor it if he thinks that he is attacking with such inhuman cruelty rather than serving the Lord God, his creator and redeemer. Let him labor to moderate his behavior in such a way that he may be seen in everything according to his capacity rather to help than to hinder[7] his most faithful source of reward. Let him namely bestow whatever benefits he can on the more perfect, to God's praise, by which they may advance in good. And to the less perfect let him show every care that he can by which they may be corrected.[8] Moreover let him be subject[9] in devout love to his superiors in all that is good, to obey and follow them and in bearing kindly with their failings. None the less, let him not praise them in anything that is blameworthy; and anything that he cannot correct[10] by words, in so far as he can let him try faithfully to correct by constant desires and heartfelt prayers poured out to God.

[7] Cf. RB 64.8.

[8] Cf. RB 2.27–28.

[9] RB 7.34.

[10] RB 28.

CHAPTER SEVENTY-FIVE

SPIRITUAL PROFIT

1. When another person had been more devoutly entrusted to her, as was her custom while she first came to pray she was longing to win from the Lord that he would make this person a participant in all that the Lord himself would condescend to perform through her, unworthy though she was, in vigils, fasts, prayers and other works of piety. The Lord replied: 'I shall certainly share with him all the benefits that the boundless courtesy of my divinity freely works in you, and will work unto the end'. She replied: 'Since your holy universal Church is a participant in all that you condescend to perform, both in and through me (unworthy though I am) and also through your other chosen ones, what then should that person receive from your loving-kindness more specially out of all that, because I desire her with special love to become a participant in all the benefits you have bestowed on me?'

The Lord replied: 'It is like this: when a noble maiden knows how to skillfully construct varied jewels from pearls and precious stones, with which she adorns both herself and her sister, she acquires renown and respect for her father and mother and all the household. None the less she who adorns herself with necklaces and bracelets that she has made for herself, wins very great mass favor and praise, and consequently her beloved sister too, whom she has made lovely with jewels like her own (even if they are not so consummately exquisite) has greater renown than her other sisters, who are not adorned in the same way. In the same way, too, although the Church participates in the individual benefits bestowed on any of the faithful, all the same the person who receives them has the greatest profit, and consequently anyone to whom the original recipient wishes to communicate in special love also pursues greater advantage and profit from it'.

2. Then she put before the Lord that same person, who had often sustained Dame M. the chantress, of pious memory, in her sickness out of his own pocket; none the less he sorrowfully bewailed that he done her too little service. Moreover he also used to sorrow over the fact that he had spoken with her too infrequently concerning the salvation of his soul, because he was always afraid of getting in her way or tiring her. The Lord replied: 'Because of the good will with which again and again he benefited my beloved with cheerful generosity—and he would gladly have done even more—he now serves me every day at table just as an illustrious prince serves his lord the emperor. Since I take pleasure in all those services that she devoutly rendered me, with strength drawn from the benefits that were lavished on her by him in food, drink and so on, as in all the thoughts, words and deeds that ever prompted him to advance my chosen one in any needs whatsoever. But as for that failing that he bewails he has, because he spoke with her too infrequently, I myself shall make up for this like a loving bridegroom who sees his bride overscrupulous out of some feeling of misplaced delicacy, who longs greatly but dares not ask. He condescends to her embarrassment and sometimes gives two of what she longed for. Thus I shall in person make up every failing'.

3. 'In addition, on account of the joyful greeting that led him to rejoice for my chosen one with devout heart in all the benefits I bestowed on her, his soul shall receive in heaven for all eternity with inestimable pleasure the brilliance of all my benefits, which the unsearchable splendor of my divine brightness aims at her, from the soul of my bride. For just as sun shining on water makes the wall shine, so the brightness of my benefits shining in the souls of those whom I have anticipated with special benefits on

earth in the blessings of divine sweetness[1] shall for all eternity give brightness to the souls of those who rejoice with them with special joyful greeting; or rather with this much difference, just as a clean mirror reflects more precisely the image of something opposite it'.

[1] Ps 20:4.

CHAPTER SEVENTY-SIX

THE PROFIT OF TEMPTATION

1. She was praying to the Lord for a certain person suffering temptation and received this reply: 'I sent that temptation and I am allowing it so that, in recognizing and weeping over her own weakness and, by weeping, striving to vanquish it, she will be unable to do so and will be humbled. By this means her other failings that she does not recognize will be partly blotted out in my eyes. It often happens in some people that while they are examining one rather obvious stain on their hands, they wash their hands completely and in this way clean them from other dirt, although they would never have washed them at all had they not been driven to it by that more obvious stain!'

CHAPTER SEVENTY-SEVEN

THAT FREQUENT COMMUNION IS WELCOME TO GOD

1. A certain person, compelled by a zeal for righteousness, was once stirred up against certain other people whom he personally judged insufficiently prepared and devout, but who none the less went to communion quite often. This person openly opposed them and his words made some of them more fainthearted about receiving communion.

While she was praying for him she asked the Lord what he thought about this. The Lord replied: 'Since my delight is to be with the sons of men[1] and I have left them this sacrament out of my great affection in memory of me, as a constant reminder to be undertaken anew, and in addition I have bound myself through this to remain with the faithful even to the consummation of the world,[2] anyone who holds back by words or suggestions someone who is not in mortal sin interferes with or interrupts in some way my delights that I could have had in them. He is like an over-severe tutor who restrains the king's son too harshly or drags him away from the companionship and games of those his own age who are rather low-born or poor, but whose company the king's son enjoys

[1] Prv 8:31.

[2] Mt 28:20.

very much, simply because he thinks it more suitable for the young man to enjoy the honor due to royalty than to play in the streets with a stick or such like. Then she said: 'Lord, if that man made up his mind to avoid that in future, surely you would pardon him for anything he has done wrong hitherto?' The Lord replied: 'Not only would I forgive him but I would also find it as welcome as the king's son would find it if his tutor cheerfully took him back to play with his beloved contemporaries whom a little earlier he had driven off with dire severity'.

CHAPTER SEVENTY-EIGHT

THE PROFIT OF ZEAL

1. When she was praying for someone who was depressed for this reason, that she was afraid that she had once incurred guilt in the eyes of God because she was rather annoyed at the failings of certain people whose example she feared was harming the profit of the religious life and discipline, the best of teachers instructed her with these words: 'If someone desires his zeal to be a most praiseworthy sacrifice for me, and most useful profit for his own soul, he must strive for three things. First, that he should show a calmer face to that person whose faults, when humanity or necessity demand it, he is pursuing and, according to his own necessity, loving words and deeds. Second, that he should be careful not to recite those faults in some place where he cannot hope either for any amendment on the part of the guilty person or for a warning for others listening. Third, that if his conscience tells him that something needs correction in someone, he should not stay silent out of human fear, but he should search for opportunities to get rid of the faults lovingly and profitably, purely to the praise of God and the salvation of souls. And then he will certainly be rewarded in proportion to effort, not profit. For if no profit results, the damage will not be his but others', who do not agree with him or gainsay him.'

2. Similarly, she was praying for two people who were arguing with each other. It seemed that one of them thought she was

defending justice, but it seemed that the other was promoting love of neighbors. The Lord replied: 'When a kindly father sees his children playing in his presence and fighting each other for fun, he sometimes turns a blind eye and smiles. But if he sees one set upon the other more violently, he quickly gets up and rather sharply corrects the delinquent. Similarly I, the Father of mercies, turn a blind eye while I see them having slight differences of opinion while their intention is good, although I would find it more welcome that they would both enjoy complete harmony. But if one of them should act more harshly towards the other, she would certainly not be able to escape the correcting rod of my fatherly justice'.

CHAPTER SEVENTY-NINE

THE FUTURE USEFULNESS OF PRAYER

1. Another person quite often complained that she could detect no profit from the prayer of those who prayed for her. She put this to the Lord and asked him the reason. The Lord replied: 'Ask her which she judges is more useful for her little brother or some other of her relatives to whom she would very much like the benefit of some church to be given: should the church be granted him, or should the value of the church be presented to the boy all at once, while he is still at school, and it left to the boy's own judgment what he should do with the money? Since it is not reasonably possible to arrange otherwise than that it would be more useful for the boy to be granted the benefit of the church that can enrich him with many good things, when he comes to years of discretion, than the value that he would waste, as children do, and afterwards be as wretched and needy as before; therefore let her have faith in my divine loving-kindness and wisdom, that I who am her father, brother and lover, pursue and ordain the profit of her soul and body much more carefully and conscientiously than she does the interests of any relative. She can be sure that I certainly keep safe the fruit of all prayers and desires poured out to me for her salvation with most careful fidelity, until the proper predestined time. Then I shall pour them all out at once when they cannot be vitiated or diminished

by anyone's untimely behavior. And let her believe that this is far more healthy for her than for me to pour out, immediately after a prayer has been offered for her, some consolation that perhaps vanity would cloud or pride would shrivel up, or even that I should grant her earthly prosperity that could be the occasion of various moral disasters'.

CHAPTER EIGHTY

THE PROFIT OF OBEDIENCE

1. While the hebdomadary was reciting the chapter by heart at Matins, it was revealed to [Gertrud] that she was doing this according to the precept of the Rule that says reading should be recited from memory, and so she was acquiring such merit from this as if there were as many people standing in God's presence, praying for her, as there were words that she had labored to declare. From this she understood that at the hour of death, when according to Bernard his deeds, as it were, say to the anxious man: 'You performed us; we are your deeds; we will not desert you but will always be with you and go with you to the judgment;'[1] then by the favor of God all acts of obedience, like noble men and women, shall comfort him and intercede for him to God, so that any good deed, performed out of obedience with right intention, shall win a person remission for some negligence. And this will be a great source of comfort to the person in his death agony.

[1] Pseudo-Bernard, *Meditationes Piissimae* 2:5 (PL 184:488B).

CHAPTER EIGHTY-ONE

COMMENDATION OF THE HEBDOMADARY'S RECITATION OF THE PSALTER

1. Similarly, another hebdomadary who was about to read the Psalter set for the community had asked [Gertrud] to pray for her. While she was doing so she saw in spirit the Son of God taking that hebdomadary up with him before the throne of God the Father and praying his heavenly Father to give her the intention of faithfulness and of that love by which the Son of God himself had desired the praise of God the Father and the salvation of the human race, to help her to gain all her desires. And when the Son had prayed to the High Father, that person for whom she had prayed was seen to be dressed in garments like his.

Just as the Son of God is said to stand before the Father, pleading for the Church, so she also stood before the Lord God the Father with his Son like Queen Esther on behalf of her people, that is, praying for her own community. And when she performed the set parts of the Psalter in this state, the heavenly Father welcomed every single word from her in two ways: that is, like a lord who welcomes from a vassal the fact that he has himself discharged debts on the debtors' behalf, and who allows his steward money to take away to distribute to his dearest friends. For the Lord seemed at that moment to present to the person who has been frequently mentioned all that she longed to win for the community by her prayers, and also set her before him to reach out to the other members of the community whenever someone drew near to pray for them.

CHAPTER EIGHTY-TWO

THE USEFULNESS OF SUBJECTION

1. When she was praying for a certain office holder's failing, that the Lord would correct it, she received this answer: 'Do you not know that not only that person but also all those who hold authority in this my beloved community are not without certain failings? Since no one can live in this world who is completely faultless, I allow this from the abundance of my divine loving-kindness, sweetness and love, that led me to choose this community so that from this its merit might be wonderfully enhanced. For it is a much greater virtue to be subject to one whose failings are known than to another whose deeds seem beyond reproach in every way'. When she replied: 'Although, my Lord, I rejoice in the merits of the subordinates, nevertheless I still long for the superiors to be without the blame that, I am afraid, they sometimes incur from their failing', the Lord replied: 'I knew all their failings that now become obvious from the varied nature of their responsibilities; but at that time perhaps they would never achieve such great humility. And for this reason just as the merit of the subordinates increases from both their [superiors'] strengths and their failings, so also the merit of the superiors increases from the failings as well as the successes of their subordinates, in the way that in a single body the various members all work for the profit of all'. From these words she understood how much the loving-kindness of the divine wisdom overflows,

and how subtly it provides for the salvation of the chosen when it allows failings to exist in order to lead on to greater successes; so much so that it seemed to her that if the goodness of God had never shone in anything except this alone, every created being would be unable to praise him worthily.

CHAPTER EIGHTY-THREE

THE FAITHFUL PURGATION OF A PERSON

1. Again, she was praying for someone who was depressed and received this answer: 'Do not lose faith: I do not allow my chosen to be burdened in any way beyond their capacity, and I am also with them, weighing due measure. Just as a mother, when she wants to warm her child at the fire, always holds her hand between the fire and the child, so I who know what is suitable to purge my chosen through tribulation, do not do this to burn them up but rather to test them and save them'.

2. She was praying for someone whom she saw lacking in desire and said among other things: 'Lord, since I, though the least of your creatures, none the less pray for that person to your praise, and you are so all-powerful that you can do everything, why do you not hear me?' The Lord replied: 'Just as I have the power to do all things from my omnipotence, so I discern all things from my unsearchable wisdom. Nor do I do anything that is not fitting. Just as an earthly king who has a force of willing troops,[1] when he wants to have his stable purged none the less does not by any means do it with his own hands as it would not be fitting, so I turn no one

[1] *potentiam tam virium quam voluntatum.*

from the evil into which he has fallen voluntarily unless he himself forces himself,[2] changes his will, and shows himself to me as fit and proper'.

[2] *vim inferens.*

CHAPTER EIGHTY-FOUR

THE LORD'S PROVISION FOR A PERSON

1. Once she was thinking about someone who during Matins walked around the choir and warned others on observing certain points that sometimes cause confusion from forgetfulness during the divine office. She asked the Lord how he would welcome such eagerness. The Lord replied: 'If someone is eager to forestall negligence in the divine office for my praise, and also to warn others for the same purpose, I shall provide for him anything that he has himself neglected in due devotion and intention'.

CHAPTER EIGHTY-FIVE

THE OFFERING UP OF BURDENS

1. When she was praying for someone who was burdened by the sickness of one of her close friends whom she was afraid she would shortly lose, she was taught by the Lord with these words: 'When a person is afraid to lose, or has lost, a beloved friend in whom he found not only the comfort of friendship but also encouragement for his soul's profit; if he whole-heartedly offers me that burden he feels in his heart—even to the extent that if he could keep his friend he would of his own accord be willing to do without him for my praise, choosing that my will should be accomplished in losing his friend rather than his own will in keeping the friend; he must be sure, when he can bend his heart to such a wish for as little as a single hour, that after that time my kindness will always preserve that offering in the same perfect noble state that it had in his heart at that hour. And every burden from human weakness that he bears in future will work together with that one for the profit of his eternal salvation, so much so that every single thought that burdens his heart—for instance, when he thinks, 'You could have this or that comfort, or help, or relief, from that person whom you now have to do without'—such thoughts, I say, and others like them that overburden a person from human weakness have the effect in his soul of preparing a place there for divine comfort, after he has made that offering. For I truly wish to pour into that soul as many comforts as the burdensome thoughts that he allows to come upon

his heart, after he has made the offering I have described. From this, as if from necessity, I am constrained by my own goodness and I do not hesitate to will it, just as a craftsman ought to set in the masterpiece he has made from gold or silver as many jewels as there are sockets he has prepared earlier for gems. My divine consolation is equal to jewels, for certain jewels are said to have powers. Similarly, any divine consolation that a person couples together with a transitory burden is of such great virtue that no person could ever lose anything so great that my divine consolation could not restore it a hundred times over[1] in this life, and a thousand times in the life to come'.

[1]Mt 19:29; Mk 10:30.

CHAPTER EIGHTY-SIX

THE BLEMISHING OF VIRGINITY

1. Another time she was praying for someone who greatly desired to possess the reward of virginity in the sight of the Lord, but was afraid she had at some time incurred some blemish from human weakness. That person appeared in the Lord's embrace, dressed in snowy-white robes that were styled with clumsy folds. Hence she was taught by the Lord with these words: 'When virginity has contracted a blemish from human weakness and a person has achieved true penitence for it, my kindliness allots to the soul a style in which those stains on her virginity appear styled like the folds in a garment. None the less, as the words of Scripture cannot be altered that say: 'Incorruptibility brings near to God',[1] these same stains could be contracted from such great sins that they would in part impede the sweetness of divine love, just as garments with many thick folds to a certain extent separate the bride from the bridegroom's embraces'.

[1] Ws 6:20.

CHAPTER EIGHTY-SEVEN

THE BARRIER OF ONE'S OWN OPINION

1. Similarly, while she was praying for someone who desired to obtain the grace of divine consolation, she received this reply from the Lord: 'That woman has a barrier that cannot admit the sweetness of my grace. For when I attract my chosen ones to me by the faint breath of the taste of intimate love, anyone stubbornly set in her own opinion creates a barrier like that a man creates who buries his nose in his cloak so as not to catch the sweet fragrance of exotic scents. But if anyone, by renouncing his own opinion for love of me, follows another's opinion, the more difficulty he has in denying himself, the more greatly his reward is increased. For there is in this not only humility but also the power of victory. And so the apostle says: "He shall not be crowned unless he has striven lawfully" '.[1]

[1] 2 Tm 2:5.

CHAPTER EIGHTY-EIGHT

THAT THE WILL IS TAKEN FOR THE DEED

1. When praying for someone who was greatly depressed by a certain task enjoined on her, she was instructed by the Lord with this answer: 'If someone is willing for my sake to undertake a somewhat onerous task and in which he also fears some barrier that he fears will result in harm to his prayer-life, and he still disregards that harm to his own soul so that he may fulfill my will; I value that will so greatly that I take the intention alone as if it were the completed act, even if it never reaches the stage that the person even begins this task. None the less it has such fruit in my eyes as if he had completed the whole task and had in the meantime avoided all negligence'.

CHAPTER EIGHTY-NINE

THAT OUTER THINGS SHOULD NOT BE PREFERRED TO INNER

1. When she was praying for another person who was often burdened by various things that depended on her advice, she received this reply: 'Through burdens I purge that negligence by which, in feeling too humanly in this, she to a certain extent preferred outer usefulness to inner progress'. She replied: 'Since we cannot exist without the help of outer goods, what sin did she commit in attending to them, as it particularly concerned her? ' The Lord replied: 'It is a noble and beautiful honor for a maiden to have various fur linings under her cloak; but if she turns them inside out, what had earlier been a source of honor and beauty becomes quite the opposite, a source of disgrace and embarrassment. And so if there is no other way the girl's mother, not allowing her daughter to become a laughing-stock, will at least cover her with another garment lest she be thought crazy. In the same way I, too, tenderly loving this daughter of mine, cover her failing with various burdens that I quite often allow to fall to her lot, for the same reason, through no fault of her own. And in addition through her patience I adorn her with a special jewel. For I have commanded in the gospel that one should first, that is principally, seek the kingdom of God and its righteousness,[1] that is,

[1]Lk 12:31.

progress in inner things. And thence outer things should not even be sought secondarily, but rather I have promised that they will be added'.

Any religious should weigh the value of that saying with particular care, who desires to be God's special friend.

INDEX OF SCRIPTURAL REFERENCES

Numbers refer to the pages of the text.

GENERAL INDEX

CISTERCIAN TEXTS

Bernard of Clairvaux

- Apologia to Abbot William
- Five Books on Consideration: Advice to a Pope
- Homilies in Praise of the Blessed Virgin Mary
- Letters of Bernard of Clairvaux / by B.S. James
- Life and Death of Saint Malachy the Irishman
- Love without Measure: Extracts from the Writings of St Bernard / by Paul Dimier
- On Grace and Free Choice
- On Loving God / Analysis by Emero Stiegman
- Parables and Sentences
- Sermons for the Summer Season
- Sermons on Conversion
- Sermons on the Song of Songs I–IV
- The Steps of Humility and Pride

William of Saint Thierry

- The Enigma of Faith
- Exposition on the Epistle to the Romans
- Exposition on the Song of Songs
- The Golden Epistle
- The Mirror of Faith
- The Nature and Dignity of Love
- On Contemplating God: Prayer & Meditations

Aelred of Rievaulx

- Dialogue on the Soul
- Liturgical Sermons, I
- The Mirror of Charity
- Spiritual Friendship
- Treatises I: On Jesus at the Age of Twelve, Rule for a Recluse, The Pastoral Prayer
- Walter Daniel: The Life of Aelred of Rievaulx

John of Ford

- Sermons on the Final Verses of the Songs of Songs I–VII

Gilbert of Hoyland

- Sermons on the Songs of Songs I–III
- Treatises, Sermons and Epistles

Other Early Cistercian Writers

- Adam of Perseigne, Letters of
- Alan of Lille: The Art of Preaching
- Amadeus of Lausanne: Homilies in Praise of Blessed Mary
- Baldwin of Ford: Spiritual Tractates I–II
- Gertrud the Great: Spiritual Exercises
- Gertrud the Great: The Herald of God's Loving-Kindness (Books 1, 2)
- Gertrud the Great: The Herald of God's
- Guerric of Igny: Liturgical Sermons I
- Helinand of Froidmont: Verses on Death
- Idung of Prüfening: Cistercians and Cluniacs: The Case for Cîteaux
- Isaac of Stella: Sermons on the Christian Year, I–[II]
- The Life of Beatrice of Nazareth
- Serlo of Wilton & Serlo of Savigny: Seven Unpublished Works
- Stephen of Lexington: Letters from Ireland
- Stephen of Sawley: Treatises

MONASTIC TEXTS

Eastern Monastic Tradition

- Besa: The Life of Shenoute
- Cyril of Scythopolis: Lives of the Monks of Palestine
- Dorotheos of Gaza: Discourses and Sayings
- Evagrius Ponticus: Praktikos and Chapters on Prayer
- Handmaids of the Lord: Lives of Holy Women in Late Antiquity & the Early Middle Ages / by Joan Petersen
- Harlots of the Desert / by Benedicta Ward
- John Moschos: The Spiritual Meadow
- Lives of the Desert Fathers
- Lives of Simeon Stylites / by Robert Doran
- The Luminous Eye / by Sebastian Brock
- Mena of Nikiou: Isaac of Alexandra & St Macrobius
- Pachomian Koinonia I–III (Armand Veilleux)
- Paphnutius: Histories/Monks of Upper Egypt
- The Sayings of the Desert Fathers / by Benedicta Ward
- Spiritual Direction in the Early Christian East / by Irénée Hausherr
- The Spiritually Beneficial Tales of Paul, Bishop of Monembasia / by John Wortley
- Symeon the New Theologian: TheTheological and Practical Treatises & The Three Theological Discourses / by Paul McGuckin
- Theodoret of Cyrrhus: A History of the Monks of Syria
- The Syriac Fathers on Prayer and the Spiritual Life / by Sebastian Brock

CISTERCIAN PUBLICATIONS

TITLES LISTING

Western Monastic Tradition

- Anselm of Canterbury: Letters I–III / by Walter Fröhlich
- Bede: Commentary…Acts of the Apostles
- Bede: Commentary…Seven Catholic Epistles
- Bede: Homilies on the Gospels I–II
- Bede: Excerpts from the Works of St Augustine on the Lettrs of the Blessed Apostle Paul
- The Celtic Monk / by U. Ó Maidín
- Life of the Jura Fathers
- Maxims of Stephen of Muret
- Peter of Celle: Selected Works
- Letters of Rancé I–II
- Rule of the Master
- Rule of Saint Augustine

Christian Spirituality

- The Cloud of Witnesses: The Development of Christian Doctrine / by David N. Bell
- The Call of Wild Geese / by Matthew Kelty
- The Cistercian Way / by André Louf
- The Contemplative Path
- Drinking From the Hidden Fountain / by Thomas Špidlík
- Eros and Allegory: Medieval Exegesis of the Song of Songs / by Denys Turner
- Fathers Talking / by Aelred Squire
- Friendship and Community / by Brian McGuire
- Gregory the Great: Forty Gospel Homilies
- High King of Heaven / by Benedicta Word
- The Hermitage Within / by a Monk
- Life of St Mary Magdalene and of Her Sister St Martha / by David Mycoff
- Many Mansions / by David N. Bell
- Mercy in Weakness / by André Louf
- The Name of Jesus / by Irénée Hausherr
- No Moment Too Small / by Norvene Vest
- Penthos: The Doctrine of Compunction in the Christian East / by Irénée Hausherr
- Praying the Word / by Enzo Bianchi
- Rancé and the Trappist Legacy / by A. J. Krailsheimer
- Russian Mystics / by Sergius Bolshakoff
- Sermons in a Monastery / by Matthew Kelty
- Silent Herald of Unity: The Life of Maria Gabrielle Sagheddu / by Martha Driscoll
- The Spirituality of the Christian East / by Thomas Špidlík
- The Spirituality of the Medieval West / by André Vauchez
- Tuning In To Grace / by André Louf
- Wholly Animals: A Book of Beastly Tales / by David N. Bell

MONASTIC STUDIES

- Community and Abbot in the Rule of St Benedict I–II / by Adalbert de Vogüé
- The Finances of the Cistercian Order in the Fourteenth Century / by Peter King
- Fountains Abbey and Its Benefactors / by Joan Wardrop
- The Hermit Monks of Grandmont / by Carole A. Hutchison
- In the Unity of the Holy Spirit / by Sighard Kleiner
- The Joy of Learning & the Love of God: Essays in Honor of Jean Leclercq
- Monastic Odyssey / by Marie Kervingant
- Monastic Practices / by Charles Cummings
- The Occupation of Celtic Sites in Ireland / by Geraldine Carville
- Reading St Benedict / by Adalbert de Vogüé
- Rule of St Benedict: A Doctrinal and Spiritual Commentary / by Adalbert de Vogüé
- The Rule of St Benedict / by Br. Pinocchio
- St Hugh of Lincoln / by David H. Farmer
- The Venerable Bede / by Benedicta Ward
- What Nuns Read / by David N. Bell
- With Greater Liberty: A Short History of Christian Monasticism & Religious Orders / by Karl Frank

CISTERCIAN STUDIES

- Aelred of Rievaulx: A Study / by Aelred Squire
- Athirst for God: Spiritual Desire in Bernard of Clairvaux's Sermons on the Song of Songs / by Michael Casey
- Beatrice of Nazareth in Her Context / by Roger De Ganck
- Bernard of Clairvaux: Man, Monk, Mystic / by Michael Casey [tapes and readings]
- Bernardus Magister...Nonacentenary
- Catalogue of Manuscripts in the Obrecht Collection of the Institute of Cistercian Studies / by Anna Kirkwood
- Christ the Way: The Christology of Guerric of Igny / by John Morson
- The Cistercians in Denmark / by Brian McGuire
- The Cistercians in Scandinavia / by James France
- A Difficult Saint / by Brian McGuire
- A Gathering of Friends: Learning & Spirituality in John of Ford / by Costello and Holdsworth
- Image and Likeness: Augustinian Spirituality of William of St Thierry / by David Bell

- Index of Authors & Works in Cistercian Libraries in Great Britain I / by David Bell
- Index of Cistercian Authors and Works in Medieval Library Catalogues in Great Britian / by David Bell
- The Mystical Theology of St Bernard / by Étienne Gilson
- The New Monastery: Texts & Studies on the Earliest Cistercians
- Nicolas Cotheret's Annals of Cîteaux / by Louis J. Lekai
- Pater Bernhardus: Mentor of Martin Luther... / by Franz Posset
- A Second Look at Saint Bernard / by Jean Leclercq
- The Spiritual Teachings of St Bernard of Clairvaux / by John R. Sommerfeldt
- Studies in Medieval Cistercian History
- Studiosorum Speculum / by Louis J. Lekai
- Three Founders of Cîteaux / by Jean-Baptiste Van Damme
- Towards Unification with God (Beatrice of Nazareth in Her Context, 2)
- William, Abbot of St Thierry
- Women and St Bernard of Clairvaux / by Jean Leclercq

MEDIEVAL RELIGIOUS WOMEN

edited by Lillian Thomas Shank and John A. Nichols:

- Distant Echoes
- Hidden Springs: Cistercian Monastic Women (2 volumes)
- Peace Weavers

CARTHUSIAN TRADITION

- The Call of Silent Love / by A Carthusian
- The Freedom of Obedience / by A Carthusian
- Guigo II: The Ladder of Monks & Twelve Meditations / by Colledge & Walsh
- Halfway to Heaven / by R.B. Lockhart
- Interior Prayer / by A Carthusian
- Meditations of Guigo II / by A. Gordon Mursall
- Prayer of Love and Silence / by A Carthusian
- Poor, Therefore Rich / by A Carthusian
- They Speak by Silences / by A Carthusian
- The Way of Silent Love (A Carthusian Miscellany)
- Where Silence is Praise / by A Carthusian
- The Wound of Love (A Carthusian Miscellany)

CISTERCIAN ART, ARCHITECTURE & MUSIC

- Cistercian Abbeys of Britain
- Cistercians in Medieval Art / by James France
- Studies in Medieval Art and Architecture / edited by Meredith Parsons Lillich *(Volumes II–V are now available)*
- Stones Laid Before the Lord / by Anselme Dimier
- Treasures Old and New: Nine Centuries of Cistercian Music (compact disc)

THOMAS MERTON

- The Climate of Monastic Prayer / by T. Merton
- Legacy of Thomas Merton / by P. Hart
- Message of Thomas Merton / by P. Hart
- Monastic Journey of Thomas Merton / by P. Hart
- Thomas Merton/Monk / by P. Hart
- Thomas Merton on St Bernard
- Toward an Integrated Humanity / edited by M. Basil Pennington

CISTERCIAN LITURGICAL DOCUMENTS SERIES

- Cistercian Liturgical Documents Series / edited by Chrysogonus Waddell, ocso
- Hymn Collection of the...Paraclete
- *Institutiones nostrae:* The Paraclete Statutes
- Molesme Summer-Season Breviary (4 volumes)
- Old French Ordinary & Breviary of the Abbey of the Paraclete (2 volumes)
- Twelfth-century Cistercian Hymnal (2 volumes)
- The Twelfth-century Cistercian Psalter
- Two Early Cistercian *Libelli Missarum*

STUDIA PATRISTICA

- Studia Patristica XVIII, Volumes 1, 2 and 3

CISTERCIAN PUBLICATIONS

HOW TO CONTACT US

Editorial Queries

Editorial queries & advance book information should be directed to the Editorial Offices:

- Cistercian Publications
  WMU Station
  1201 Oliver Street
  Kalamazoo, Michigan 49008

- Telephone 616 387 8920
- Fax 616 387 8921

How to Order in the United States

Customers may order these books through booksellers or directly by contacting the warehouse at the address below:

- Cistercian Publications
  Saint Joseph's Abbey
  167 North Spencer Road
  Spencer, Massachusetts 01562-1233

- Telephone 508 885 8730
- Fax 508 885 4687
- e-mail cistpub@spencerabbey.org
- Web Site www.spencerabbey.org/cistpub

How to Order from Canada

- Novalis
  49 Front Street East, Second Floor
  Toronto, Ontario M5E 1B3

- Telephone 416 363 3303
  1 800 387 7164
- Fax 416 363 9409

How to Order from Europe

- Cistercian Publications
  Mount Saint Bernard Abbey
  Coalville, Leicester LE67 5UL

- Fax 44 1530 81 46 08

Cistercian Publications is a non-profit corporation. Its publishing program is restricted to monastic texts in translation and books on the monastic tradition.

A complete catalogue of texts in translation and studies on early, medieval, and modern monasticism is available, free of charge, from any of the addresses above.